STUDY SKILLS

MACMILLAN MASTER SERIES

Basic Management
Biology
Chemistry
Commerce
Computer Programming
Computers
Data Processing
Economics
Electronics
English Language
French
German
Italian
Marketing
Mathematics
Modern World History
Office Practice
Physics
Principles of Accounts
Sociology
Spanish
Statistics
Study Skills

MASTERING
STUDY SKILLS

R. FREEMAN

First edition 1982
Reprinted 1982

Published by
THE MACMILLAN PRESS LTD
Companies and representatives
throughout the world

Typeset by
Reproduction Drawings Ltd, Sutton, Surrey

Printed and bound by
Unwin Brothers Ltd.
The Gresham Press,
Old Woking, Surrey

ISBN 0 333 31298 8 (hard cover)
ISBN 0 333 30448 9 (paper cover editions: U.K. and export)

CONTENTS

CONTENTS

PREFACE

Mastering Study Skills is specially written for students who find the processes of study difficult. Many people have difficulty in remembering things or are mystified by the process of writing an essay. All too easily students accept that they can't do these things because they are just poor students. Yet usually the reason for their difficulties is simply that they never actually learnt how to memorise, how to make notes, or how to write an essay. This book teaches just those skills.

Mastering Study Skills is not, however, just a book which tells you about how to learn. Such books exist but you won't improve your learning skills by reading such books any more than you will play better tennis by reading a book about tennis playing. *Mastering Study Skills* is a *course*. That is it's a book you have to work at through carrying out its numerous activities which both explore your current range of study skills and give you practice in acquiring new ones.

By the end of the book you will not only know more about effective study techniques but you will have put into practice new approaches to planning and timetabling, memory, understanding, notetaking, essay-writing and examination technique.

Richard Freeman

ACKNOWLEDGEMENTS

The author and publishers wish to thank the following, who have kindly given permission for the use of copyright material:

George Allen & Unwin (Publishers) Ltd for an extract from *Authority and the Individual* by Bertrand Russell.

Guardian Newspapers Ltd for extracts from issues of *The Guardian*.

London Express News and Feature Services for an extract from the *Sun* newspaper article 'Stand Firm Maggie'.

Longman Group Ltd for entry no. 705 from Roget's *Thesaurus of English Words and Phrases*.

Oxford University Press for an extract from *Karl Marx: Selected Writings*, edited by David McLellan (1977).

SAAB (Gt Britain) Ltd for an advertisement of the SAAB 900 Turbo car.

Scuola di Barbiana, Florence, for an extract from *Letter to a Teacher*.

WHERE AND HOW
TO STUDY

1.1 PLANS AND TIMETABLES

Successful students invariably have well-designed plans and timetables. (They may not have them written down, but almost certainly thay have a plan in their heads.) A plan is an overall view of the course of study and will usually cover a term or a year. A timetable is a more detailed day-to-day division of time and covers not only study but, to some extent, the other activities which are essential to your life.

Timetables are great aids to efficiency. First, they enable you to analyse the use you are making of your time. Is it the most effective scheme? Are the hours allocated to study the best ones? A timetable also takes a load off your mind. Just as listing pressing commitments (see Chapter 2) enables you to concentrate on the one task in hand, so timetabling the day's or week's routine ensures that all the decisions have been taken in advance. Without a timetable you will have to make a hundred decisions each week as you try to fit everything in. The very making of the decisions will tax your energy and leave you less ready for study.

1.2 THE WEEKLY TIMETABLE

The basic element in your planning is probably the weekly timetable. A week is a suitable period of time not only because it is the module of time used for most college timetables, but also becuase it is about as far ahead as most of us can plan with confidence.

But whether your planning period is two days, a week or a month, your timetable must be realistic. An unrealistic timetable may be worse than no timetable at all since its neatly displayed allocation of activities can deceive you into thinking that all will get done in time. So what is realistic? Well, that depends on you and all your circumstances so, for your first activity, I am going to ask you to look at the way you use your time at the moment.

First, however, let me remind you of what I said in the introduction about these activities. The activities are an essential part of the book. They make the difference between *reading* about how to study and *learning* actually *how* to study in a way which will be helpful to you. So please don't skip the activities.

● **Activity 1 How you use your time** ●
The idea behind this activity is to see how your time gets used up while you are a student so that you can later look at how it might be used differently. This activity is therefore straightforward if you are a student now but if you are about to become one it will require that you imagine the lifestyle that you expect to have as a student.

Write down how many hours a week (seven days) you spend on the following activities:

Study supervised by college
(e.g. lectures, lab work, seminars)
Private study
Travel
Eating, food preparation and food shopping
Household chores
Leisure activities
Sleeping
Other

Total

A week contains 168 hours so your list should have that total. If it hasn't, find out why not before proceeding.

What can you learn from Activity 1? Unless you are a very unusual person, you are likely to find that you can never find time for everything and that you often do not seem to have time to fit all your study into your life. Is this really because there are not enough hours in the day, or is it just a lack of organisation? Activity 2 should help you answer this.

● **Activity 2 How much time do you need?** ●
In Activity 1 you wrote down how many hours a week you currently spend on various activities. Now, using the same headings, write down how much time you think you need each week for these activities.

Study supervised by college
Private study

Travel
Eating, food preparation, food shopping
Household chores
Leisure activities
Sleeping
Other

Total

This time I hope that your total is less than 168 hours – if it isn't then you really do have a full life! But most people will find that Activity 2 shows a lot of the time used up in Activity 1 is available for reallocating.

In general you are unlikely to *need* more than 40 hours per week for study of all kinds, and Activity 2 will have shown you that within your life there is more than enough room to fit this in. How do you fit study in at the moment?

● **Activity 3 Your current timetable** ●
Table 1.1 shows a blank timetable for a week. Using the figures from Activity 2, fill in the table to show how you organise a typical week at the moment.

Table 1.1 **Your present timetable**

	12 pm	1 am	2	3	4	5	6	7	8	9	10	11	12 pm	1	2	3	4	5	6	7	8	9	10	11
Sun																								
Mon																								
Tue																								
Wed																								
Thu																								
Fri																								
Sat																								

1.3 HOW LONG SHOULD STUDY PERIODS BE?

(a) How many hours per week?
You may feel that your current timetable suits you very well. Perhaps you not only manage to complete all the study that you need to but also find that you work efficiently without taking up too much time. But if you are not in this happy position, then you may need to reconsider the best way to use the time that you have.

For all students there are two limiting factors on the amount of time they should devote to study. The first is that periods of less than half an hour are of little use. Any study activity involves a warming-up period during which your efficiency is low. All you can hope to do with these short periods is to use them for odd activities like sorting notes or checking booklists. Thus, if at all possible, you should aim to make your study periods at least an hour. If your study is going to involve writing essays, you will need 1-2-hour study sessions for this purpose. For note-taking, reading, exercises and so on, periods of an hour will be useful. The second limiting factor is the maximum number of hours you can expect to put in in one day. Experiments show that you cannot expect to study efficiently for more than three hours without a substantial break. Nor can you expect to work for more than eight hours in any one day. Full-time students should aim at around 35–45 hours of study a week, including lectures, laboratory work and so on. Part-time and home-study students can't hope to aim at this level, and for them 10 hours per week is likely to be the upper limit.

The total hours should be spent as evenly as possible over five or six days of the week. You will learn more working for one hour a day, six days a week, than working six hours on one day of the week. The regular study reinforces what was learnt the previous day before it is forgotten. (See Section 2.2.)

Not only should study be evenly spaced through the week, but it should be evenly spaced through the year. Massive cramming sessions are not effective and long hours only lead to inefficiency. After Dunkirk, the British war factories increased working hours from 8 to 11 or 12 hours a day. Production rose dramatically in the first week of the crisis period, but within five weeks production had fallen back to the pre-Dunkirk level despite the continued working of extra hours. Excessive hours simply lead to inefficiency and bad health.

(b) One day's study

Ideally, study hours should come early in the day when attention and concentration are at their peak. The highest output is usually attained in the second hour of study in the morning. For most correspondence and part-time students, evenings provide the only opportunity for study. In such circumstances you have to make the best possible use of what free time you have.

The most difficult parts of your work should be reserved for your best study times. If, despite this, you are still reluctant to get down to a particularly difficult piece of study, start one of your prime sessions with a

'Massive cramming sessions are not effective and long hours only lead to inefficiency'

short but easy job. Switch to the more difficult task immediately after this warming-up exercise.

Each study session should start with a revision of the previous day's study, provided they follow on from one another. This reinforces the previous day's work and acts as a warming-up session.

One's efficiency and concentration tend to flag after an hour's study but they are easily revived by a short break. For maximum effect, the break should be very definite – going to a different room; taking a short walk; talking to someone. Five to ten minutes is sufficient to restore you to full efficiency.

> ● Activity 4 A typical day's study ●
> In Activity 3 you drew up a timetable of how you organise your life at present. Does the material in this section now lead you to want to use your time differently? If so, draw up a plan for a typical day's study for yourself. Take full account of other commitments and of likely distractions at different times of day.

1.4 RELAXATION

Relaxation should be an important part of your timetable. Without adequate sleep, recreation and relaxation your mind will not function efficiently. You should, therefore, make a definite point of including recreation and relaxation in your timetable. Sleep should also be counted into your plan so that you do not neglect its vital contribution to health. The independent student with a full-time job needs to pay particular attention to these points, since even 10 hours study per week is a considerable extra strain on his energies.

Students at college should try to plan their sleep and recreation to fit the general pattern of college life. In this way, other people's recreation will not clash with your studies. If you are trying to study when others are enjoying social activities, you may find the distraction too much for you. Common study hours reduce the distractions for each and every student.

As far as possible you should regard both plan and timetable as commands to be obeyed as a top priority. Only with very good reason (e.g. illness) should you depart from your plan. But the plan itself must have some flexibility. Everyone's schedules go wrong from time to time. With a workable plan you can probably get back on schedule. With a less workable plan the lack of flexibility will mean you must scrap the plan and devise a new one. A plan which you can't keep to is worse than no plan at all.

> **When to study summary**
> 1. Plan the week's study ahead.
> 2. Plan a study session for each of five or six days a week.
> 3. Sessions should be from one to three hours.
> 4. Have a definite break every hour.
> 5. Avoid late hours.
> 6. Plan recreation and relaxation into your timetable.

1.5 WHERE TO STUDY

The choice of where you study may be just as critical as the question of when to study. There are *some* people who can switch concentration on and off at will. There are others who seem to be able to work halfway up mountains or in bus shelters. But most people find study easier in surroundings which are functional and comfortable. This means trying to arrange for:

(a) A room in which you can study and be away from other distractions. Distractions can be dynamic (noise, movement) or static (radio waiting to be turned on, newspaper lying around to be read). The best way to avoid these is to reserve a special room for study or to use a bedroom as a study/ bedroom since bedrooms are rarely used in study hours and contain few distractions. On the whole libraries are not suitable places for study. There are many strange people to watch, there is constant movement and except in a few modern libraries, surfaces such as floors and desks are of a noisy variety. But for some people libraries offer the only escape from excessive home distractions. This particularly applies to families with young children.

A study room needs to be comfortable, which means first of all that it needs to be warm (about 70°F, 21°C) and well ventilated. If it is too hot or too cold, your mind will be distracted by the heat or cold of your body. It if is insufficiently ventilated, it will become stuffy and you will become drowsy and will possibly develop a headache. You will also need adequate light – day or artificial – on your working surface.

(b) A suitable desk and chair. The normal height for a writing surface is 2 ft 6 in. (750 mm) and for a typing surface is 2 ft 2 in. (650 mm). The desk top should be at least 3 ft 6 in. (1000 mm) by 1 ft 8 in. (480 mm).

Even if you can't devote a whole room to study, you should try and keep a corner somewhere where all your study materials are together. This saves no end of time which can easily be wasted in searching for pens, notepads, books etc. There are also great psychological advantages to be gained from a fixed place to study. You will come to associate the place with study so that merely entering the room or sitting at the desk will induce a favourable attitude to study.

Provided you have the space you should include a bookcase and a display board near your desk. You will need a bookcase not only to keep your books in, but to keep them together and near your work place. A display board will prove invaluable for charts, timetables and diagrams. It helps to keep more material in front of you without cluttering your desk.

● **Activity 5 Which study conditions best suit you?** ●

Not all factors that I have discussed are equally critical for all students. Try and work out which affect you most by answering these questions. In the past, when you have found your study is going well:

    (i) at what times of day have you mostly been studying?

   (ii) how long have your study periods been?

   (iii) where have you been studying?

   (iv) have any special facilities or circumstances helped your study at these times?

Where to study summary
1. Always in the same place.
2. Choose a warm, light, well ventilated room.
3. Away from other distractions.
4. Properly furnished for the job.

1.6 CHECKLIST

You should now find that you have:

   (a) analysed your present pattern of weekly activities;

   (b) worked out how much time you need for each activity;

   (c) looked at your present study timetable and replanned it to include all your essential activities;

   (d) study periods on your new timetable of sensible lengths;

   (e) described when and where you study best and taken some action to be able to study in this way in the future.

CHAPTER 2

LEARNING EFFICIENTLY

2.1 ATTENTION AND INTEREST

If you are going to learn efficiently, you must concentrate your attention on the subject to be studied. Attention is always with us. All the time your brain is receiving ever-changing stimuli – noises, seeing things move, messages from your body (hunger, cold, being uncomfortable, etc.) and you pay attention to each in turn. Normally you only attend to any one stimulus for a few seconds.

> ● **Activity 1 Are you being distracted?** ●
> Are you finding it easy to concentrate at the moment? Or is something distracting you? Write down a list of everything that is distracting you at the moment. (If nothing is distracting you at the moment, write down a list of the things that sometimes distract you when you are studying.)

Now when you want to study, you are choosing to pay attention to one thing – the piece of work to be studied. Thus you should start by ridding yourself of these distractions. Some are easy to remove, simply the right choice of where and when to study. Others are more difficult. For example, you can easily get away from the distraction of other members of the family by choosing a different room. But what if you are worrying about one member of the family? To eliminate this sort of distraction is more difficult. Try, for a start, to avoid coming to study after some other excitement such as an argument or discussion. The quieter your mind, the easier it will be to attend to your studies.

You may also have a lot of other things to attend to. They won't get done simply by worrying about them when you are studying. The best way to deal with these is by a list or a timetable, which you should have done in Chapter 1. Your work timetable settles in a general way when you are going to study. Having decided this, note down when you are going to do the other things now on your mind – like the shopping or going round to see Grandfather. This simple listing or timetable invariably satisfies you that everything will be done in due time. Then your mind clears and is ready to concentrate on studying

Even when you have cleared your mind and settled down to study, other thoughts will attract your attention from time to time. You must try and suppress these and a useful method is to work at a fair speed. Since attention can only be maintained on any one point for a few seconds, attempting to concentrate too long on one point invariably invites a stray throught to grab your attention. By working faster you keep switching your attention from one point to another, but all the points are relevant to your studies.

Interest naturally leads to attention. No one will make a good job of studying what doesn't interest him. You can maintain interest in various ways. First, use lots of sources of ideas and information. This helps to give you plenty of viewpoints on a subject and keeps your interest aroused. Second, don't try to learn a subject in isolation (see Section 2.6, on rote learning and understanding, below). Try to relate the subject all the time to everyday life and in particular to your own life. This is particularly successful if your studies are related to your job.

Of course there will be times when it is essential to master a particular point in which you just can't rouse any interest. Don't funk these points. Tackle them head-on by reserving one of your best study times (usually early in the day) for an onslaught on this point.

Attention and interest summary
1. Remove irrelevant and unwanted stimuli, e.g. noise, hunger, cold.
2. Put aside other pressing matters by listing or timetabling them.
3. Suppress unwanted thoughts by quickly switching to topic under study.
4. Understand what you are studying.
5. Take a lively interest in the subject outside your study hours.

● **Activity 2 Using what you have learnt** ●
What action have you taken to put this section into practice? Make a note of what you have done to remind yourself of the importance of this 'clearing the decks' activity.

2.2 MEMORY

(a) Learning and forgetting
Almost any student would agree that one of his main difficulties is remembering what he has once learnt. It is therefore very surprising that university

and college courses contain no advice on how to remember and how to improve recall of information. Here a knowledge of just a little psychology can be very helpful.

First let us look at learning. Most people, when learning a new subject, go through four characteristic phases illustrated in Figure 2.1.

Fig 2.1 *the learning curve*

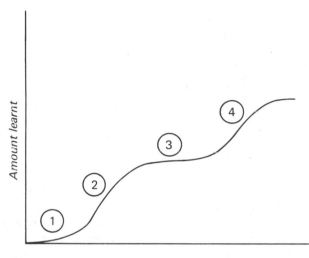

time

At stage 1, little progress is made because the subject is unfamiliar to the student. Then he enters stage 2 and makes rapid progress. After stage 2, during which he learnt quite a lot of material, he enters stage 3, the plateau. Here he seems to be in the doldrums. Despite effort, no progress seems possible. This plateau is a dangerous place, since it is here that the student may feel defeated. Making little progress, he loses confidence and throws in the sponge. The plateau is the particular enemy of the home student who fails to realise that everyone reaches this sort of plateau. But if only they persevere, they eventually move on to stage 4 when once again progress is rapid as in stage 2. At the end of stage 4, the student reaches his peak in this particular topic.

Ways to speed up the learning process are discussed below but first it helps to understand something of the process of memorising.

On the whole, we find it difficult to recall events in our lives. Unless 11 May 1965 had a special significance for you, it is unlikely that you can recall a single event of that day. In other words, we quickly lose the capacity to recall events. Even at the end of one hour's lecture, most students find it difficult to recall the first half of the lecture. After two hours or so, half the lecture will have been forgotten. The forgetting curve is shown in Figure 2.2.

Fig 2.2 *the forgetting curve*

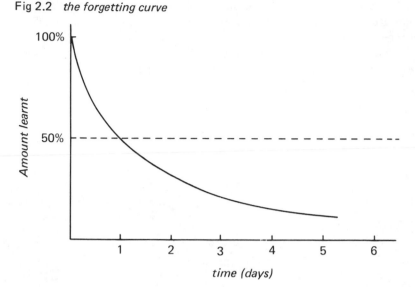

I.e. we very quickly lose half the material learnt, but after that, the decline is slow. How can this initial loss be prevented?

There are few aspects of learning of which teachers and lecturers are so ignorant as they are of memory. It is widely believed that each of us possesses a faculty called 'memory' and that some of us have better memories than others. It is also widely held that practice in memorising poems or chunks of the bible helps to develop our memories. Both these beliefs are fantasies. A person who is good at memorising material is a person with good study habits – no more and no less.

(b) Principles of memorising

● **Activity 3 What do you remember easily?** ●
Write down a list of the types of things that you find easy to remember and a list of things that you find it hard to remember.
Keep these lists ready for the end of this section.

If you were asked to memorise a line of Greek or a mathematical formula, you would, if you knew no Greek and were not a mathematician, have to memorise every twist and turn of the pen on the paper. But a Greek linguist or a mathematician would quickly learn the word or formula respectively. They would not do so because they have better memories than you. Their success is solely due to the fact that the line of Greek means something to the linguist and the mathematical formula means something to the mathematician. They memorise the material easily because (a) they understand it, and (b) it links up with other material they have learnt.

The first two rules of memory are, therefore:

(i) Never memorise something that you don't understand.

(ii) Always try to link new material with what you have previously learnt.

The next rule for memory must be taken on trust from psychology. Experiments show that if you memorise a poem, say, until you just know it, you will forget it more quickly than if you go on reciting it even after you know it perfectly. This repeated learning, even after mastery of the poem, is called overlearning.

Now memorising a poem is a very simple example. But how does one memorise the history of the Civil War? You do not learn the textbook off by heart. You use the rules of good memorising. Two are printed above. Here are two more important ones:

(iii) Select the important items to remember.

(iv) Organise the material into a meaningful system. (Advice on this comes in Section 4.1 on note-taking.)

In practice these two rules might involve making charts, diagrams, tables and so on.

Practice

Except for a few points, you will still forget material which you have once learnt. You will therefore need to go over previous work at intervals. With lecture notes, go over them as soon as possible after the lecture. If you fail to do this, they will soon become a meaningless jumble to you. With work done at home, start each session with a review of previous sessions. Once you feel the material has been mastered, you can leave the next review for four to six weeks.

Other good memory techniques

(v) Active repetition or recall such as recitation or writing out aids memorising.

(vi) The sequence of memorising should be the same as the logical sequence of the material.

(vii) Long pieces should be memorised in shorter chunks.

(viii) Where material has to be learnt by heart, rhythmic patterns help, e.g. in poetry or multiplication tables.

● **Activity 4 Do these rules apply to you?** ●

In Activity 3 you made two lists – things that you find easy to remember and things that you find hard to remember. Can you now explain to yourself why each item is in your easy or hard list?

Can you now see any ways to make it easier to remember some of the hard items?

Varieties of memorising

Not all types of learning demand so much attention to memorising as this section might imply. For example, if you are trying to understand the principle behind a particular theory, activities such as overlearning or active recall will not be of much help. It is the understanding of the principle you are trying to master - not just a bald statement of the principle. This is particularly true in mathematics, where principles are grasped through working problems which rely on these principles. Memory is, at such a time, of secondary importance. But this of course takes us back full circle to 'Never memorise something that you don't understand'.

Memory and learning summary

1. Never try to memorise what you don't understand.
2. Go over notes, reading etc. within 12 hours of writing, reading etc.
3. Master each topic before leaving it.
4. Start each session with a review of the previous session.
5. Overlearn. Don't stop when you have only just learnt something.
6. Select important points to learn.
7. Organise selected items.
8. Use active recall (recitation or writing) to aid memory.
9. Keep your material in a logical sequence.
10. Break up long pieces into manageable chunks.
11. Use rhythm when learning by heart.

● **Activity 5 Practising memory techniques** ●

Study the memory summary again. Make a list of any points which you haven't practised in the past. Keep this list handy: resolve to use it in the future.

2.3 DIFFERENCES BETWEEN LEARNERS

Most of this book is pretty dogmatic. It says 'do this', 'don't do that' and so on (although, of course, it explains why you should do this and that). Just for a moment, therefore, the differences between individuals ought to be noted.

For example, some people say they can only work with the radio on. Why, then does section 1.5 tell you not to do it? Because no one can listen to the radio and study. As already explained, attention can be directed to one thing at a time only. Thus, even those students who have the radio on are not listening to it. If it was quietly faded out, they probably wouldn't notice if they are really concentrating on their studies.

But there are some genuine differences between students. Intelligence tests reveal some intellectual differences between students but their value for adults is extremely limited. What matters is other types of personality difference of which educational tests rarely take much account. And people learn at different speeds. Your speed of learning is also affected by your previous experience and knowledge. For example, you have already met the case of memorising a Greek phrase – if you know some Greek, it is easier to memorise Greek phrases than if you know no Greek at all.

Age is another factor that can affect an individual's capacity to learn. Older people absorb new material more slowly in laboratory psychological tests. But, in voluntary studies, it is likely that older people do better because they have higher motivation. Deciding to take up 'O' level Maths at 35 is a great advantage over being forced to do it at 14.

Thus even though there are genuine individual differences in learning ability, the advice in this course should help anyone to improve his study habits. Don't be put off because you are not quite like some other student you know.

2.4 MOTIVATION, GOALS AND KNOWLEDGE OF PROGRESS

The successful student not only has good study habits and techniques, but he is highly motivated. He wants to study.

There are many different reasons for wanting to study. Universities have always placed great emphasis on learning for learning's sake – for them, being interested in the subject is sufficient motivation. But most of us have a more mundane reason for study. Quite often the reason is to get a better job. Never spurn this motive. It is one of the most powerful drives for keeping you at your studies. If you are studying for a vocational reason, try to keep it in your mind. Think about how your studies will relate to your job and career in the future.

● **Activity 6 What motivates you?** ●
Write down a list of tasks that you find easy to get down to - not just study tasks, but any activity.

Write down a second list of tasks that you find it hard to get down to.

Why do you like doing the tasks in the first list? Is there a motivational reason for each one?

Why do you not like getting down to the tasks in the second list?

This activity may have helped you to see the kinds of motivation that keep you going. In most cases the satisfaction that you got out of the task comes quite quickly and it is because there is an immediate (or not too distant) reward that the tasks are easy to start on.

This applies to study too. You need long-term aims but they are not much good for keeping you going. You also need short-term goals to keep you going week by week, day by day. For each and every study session you should set yourself definite and realistic goals. Definite in the sense that you will be able to tell at the end of the session whether or not the goal has been reached, e.g. mastering one chapter of a book. Realistic in the sense that you are aiming neither too high nor too low. Too low a goal will give you no satisfaction in achieving it; too high a goal will deprive you of the satisfaction of reaching it.

Repeated experiments have shown that students are most successful when they have a clear knowledge of their progress. You should get into the habit of checking on your progress. For example, having completed work on a chapter, quickly note down from memory the main points. Then compare them with the original chapter. Note your strengths and weaknesses and resolve to make up those weaknesses at the next study session.

Good motivation is always tied up with interest in the subject. There are many ways of livening up a subject. Try reading a book on the history of the subject. Try to find out how your subject relates to other subjects. Find out how it is used in everyday life. Look out for films and television and radio programmes connected with the subject. All these approaches will stimulate your interest and increase your motivation.

Motivation summary
1. Keep your vocational aim in mind.
2. Have clear and realistic goals for every study session.
3. Check your progress at every session.
4. Read around your subject.

● **Activity 7 Why are you using this book?** ●
Write down answers to the following questions:

What is your reason for using this book?
Can you think of any ways of increasing your motivation to study this book?

2.5 LEARNING

● **Activity 8 How fast do you learn?** ●
The following is a list of ten types of materials that you might have had to learn at one time or another. In the boxes, put a one against the item that you would find easiest to learn, a two against the next easiest and so on to the most difficult.

(a) A blank verse poem ☐
(b) Twenty words in a foreign language and their English meanings ☐
(c) A rhyming poem ☐
(d) A labelled biological diagram ☐
(e) A miscellaneous collection of objects (as in the game of 'Kim') ☐
(f) Ten telephone numbers ☐
(g) A speech from a play ☐
(h) A list of historical dates ☐
(i) The exports of half a dozen different countries ☐
(j) The birthdays of your family and friends ☐

What can you deduce from this activity? If you are like most people you will have the rhyming poem at the easy end. Why? Because it has a pattern and has clues to tell you whether or not you have remembered it correctly. On the other hand you have probably put the blank verse and the speech nearer the hard end. They are much like the rhyming poem but lack the pattern of metre and rhyme. You are also likely to have put the telephone numbers, the Kim game and the birthdays towards the hard end. Here there is no pattern and meaning. No object in a Kim game can give a clue to another object. No digit in a telephone number can give a clue to another digit. A person's name doesn't give a clue to his birthday. This therefore means that in all three cases you have to memorise by shear hard repetition.

That leaves four other types of item for which I cannot predict how hard or easy you find them. Why? Because in each case they contain material that can be understood and related to previous knowledge which you might have. So, how hard or easy you find biological diagrams depends on your knowledge of, and interest in, biology. Whether or not you find it easy to memorise historical dates depends on how much knowledge you have of history and what else you relate to those dates.

This demonstrates a very important fact about human learning: the better you understand something, the easier it is to learn. And if you don't understand something at all, you will probably find it impossible to learn.

The importance of understanding in learning cannot be emphasised enough. So much of traditional school work has laid emphasis on memorising, on copying the teacher's notes, on rehashing the teacher's specimen answers to exam questions, that we have come to associate pure memory work with learning. In the 'Memory and learning' summary box in Section 2.2 you will note that the first rule is 'Never try to memorise what you don't understand'. The first aim of any study session is understanding the topic to be studied.

Understanding is promoted by thinking about the topic. There are many different ways of doing this, some more appropriate than others to particular topics. Here are some suggestions for promoting understanding:

(i) Try to reorganise the material in the way which is best for you.

(ii) Link the new material with your previous knowledge.

(iii) Look for examples to illustrate the topic.

(iv) Look for analogies between the topic and other things.

(v) Ask: How can I apply this knowledge?

(vi) Ask: What does the author mean?

(vii) Ask: Does this new knowledge change my old ideas?

(viii) Ask: Where could this new knowledge lead? What consequences does it have?

These points will help you to understand what you read, hear or see. If you don't understand a point, you can skip it as long as you come back to it fairly soon. Quite often a 12-hour break will lead to new insight and hence to understanding. Even when you think your mind is switched off, it will think over something which really matters to you.

Understanding summary

1. Always aim for understanding.
2. Promote understanding by rearranging material, questioning the ideas and looking for links with old ideas.

2.6 ROTE LEARNING

As already mentioned, schools have frequently placed an undue emphasis on memorising material which has not been understood. Some primary school children were displaying their knowledge to a visitor and one child told him that five threes were fifteen. 'Good', he said, 'And what are three fives?' The child replied 'Oh, we haven't done the five times table yet'. Here was a child memorising multiplication tables one by one – first the two times, then the three times. But she didn't understand what multiplication was. If she had, she would have known that 5×3 is the same as 3×5.

● **Activity 9 Rote learning** ●

Here is a list of numbers. Time how long it takes you to learn the list off by heart so that you can write it down accurately in any order.

101, 37, 65, 145, 50, 5, 82, 122, 17, 10, 26

Difficult? It would be for most people since they will try to do exactly what I asked, i.e. to memorise the list. To do this is hard because the list lacks any pattern and so even when one bit is remembered it doesn't help in remembering the rest.

Now if you can give such a list a pattern, you can learn it more quickly. As it happens the list above does have a pattern and if you put the numbers into order you will notice that they are the numbers 2 to 12 multiplied by themselves with one added to each answer.

Now try a new task. Here is a list like the first one but this time I will tell you the pattern first. It is the numbers 2 to 12 multiplied by themselves with one subtracted from each answer. Time how long it takes you to learn the list until you can write it down accurately in any order. Make the maximum use that you can of knowing what the pattern is

3, 120, 143, 48, 63, 24, 35, 8, 99, 80, 15

So rote learning is difficult and slow. Does it therefore have any place in learning? Yes it does. There would be no harm in our girl learning multiplication tables by heart, provided that she first understood them. It also has a place in, say, languages. Learning vocabulary must be done by rote even if the memory is reinforced in other ways after the initial learning. For example, only rote learning will fix the Serbo-Croat for ice creams - *sladowed* - in your mind.

Take another example. Biologists have to be familiar with a very complex diagram depicting the nitrogen cycle in nature. Many biologists can draw the cycle from memory but they can also explain why it is as it is. They understand all the chemical reactions involved before they try to remember the diagram.

Whatever your subject, there may come a time when learning something by heart is both useful and sensible. But never start to memorise before you understand.

2.7 ORGANISING MATERIAL

The need to organise material to suit your own needs has already been emphasised in Section 2.2, 'Memory', and in Section 2.5, 'Learning'. Various aspects of organising such as filing and note-taking are dealt with in Sections 4.1 and 4.2. Here it is necessary to emphasise the importance of relating what you learn to yourself even while you are studying.

The organising of material should take place all the time you are studying. Merely trying to remember chapters of books will lead to failure and boredom. By putting the material in a new order, or by making up your own charts and diagrams, you will stimulate your interest and promote learning.

Most successful students who prepare for exams have a completely personal system by the time revision comes around. They have already organised their material into a form which is particularly relevant to them. Each student has his own unique system. For example, a group of students studying a period of history will each summarise the period in note form in a different way. One may prefer to use dates as key headings. Another may favour events. Another, personalities. No single method is 'best'. Each method helps the student who favours it because that is the way the student remembers history.

The way you see new material determines the way you organise it. And the way you see it is determined by all your past experience. That is why a politician of one persuasion will interpret events to favour his case, whilst a politician of another persuasion will interpret the same events to favour his, different, case. To some extent this 'setting' of attitudes is a danger in study. It prevents you from seeing new ideas. It protects you from challenges to your favourite theories and prejudices. If you happen to believe that all who draw social security benefits are 'scroungers', your attitude will sharpen you observation of 'scroungers' and blind you to the millions of honest, needy, people who draw the same benefits.

Thus you will find your mind's peculiar pattern of working both an advantage and a disadvantage. It helps you in organising new material into a form which you can easily learn and understand. It hinders you when trying to see both sides of the case and protects you from challenges to your favourite theories. Trying to overcome this disadvantage and so opening your mind to new ideas is dealt with in Sections 6.3 and 6.4.

2.8 RELATING MATERIAL TO THE OUTSIDE WORLD

We are all familiar with the fictional professor who, brilliant though he is in his subject, is a duffer in the everyday world. He can't drive a car, he doesn't know the price of bread – without his more worldly friends and relations he would be as helpless as a new-born babe. No stereotype could be further from the truth. In reality, clever people excel at more occupations than other people. Those who are good at school subjects tend to also be good at practical subjects, at sports and at mixing with people and making friends. Why?

The key to their success in life is not superior intelligence. A fair proportion of highly intelligent children turn into dull and unsuccessful adults. Similarly, many 'eleven-plus failures' obtain degrees and do well in life. The key to success is motivation and curiosity. A lot has been said about motivation in the preceding sections. But curiosity is also important. Curiosity may 'have killed the cat' but it has been the making of many successful and eminent human beings. Curiosity aids intelligent learning. It drives the learner to ask questions, to be sceptical and so to gain insight into what he learns.

Curiosity also helps you to relate what you learn to the outside world. A poor student of history learns his notes, studies his books and stops there. A good student thinks about history. He looks at buildings and relates them to their historical periods. He looks at customs and traditions and is curious about their origins. Why is the Cabinet so named? Why are Neolithic settlements rarely in the same place as modern towns? Similarly the geographer might look at population distribution, crops, transport and so on. The student of sociology or psychology might apply his subject to the behaviour of politicians or trade union leaders. The mathematician might look at the arrangement of leaves on plant stems, at the endless statistics pouring out from government and other offices, and so on.

It is by this constant application of one's subject to everyday life (and to other subjects) that one's mind learns and understands the subject. Unless you relate what you learn to everyday life, your knowledge will remain dead. You will not be able to use it. It will not benefit you in any way.

As already mentioned, those who are studying with a vocational aim should try to relate their new learning to their vocations. Keep your job in mind and ask yourself how and where your new knowledge can be used.

● **Acitivity 10 Linking what you have learnt** ●
Turn to a chapter of a textbook that you have recently studied. List the main points that are being made. Then, by the side of your first list, write down some everyday examples or applications of the points being made. For example:

Points	*Example*
Salt dissolves easily in water	There is not much salt on land – it has all dissolved in rain and run into the sea.
The nineteenth century was a period of rapid industrial growth	Look at any large, old, town that you know. Examine the size and location of its pre-nineteenth-century part. Compare with its nineteenth century buildings.

You may be just reading this chapter and writing answers to the questions posed. Can you do more? Review sections 2.6, 2.7 and 2.8. List some methods of applying these sections to this course.

Put these methods into action.

2.9 USE OF DISCUSSION TO PROMOTE LEARNING

So far all the techniques have been relevant to individual study. That is not surprising since learning is an individual process. A group can study together but they learn as individuals. Now we come to a very important method of group activity which promotes individual learning and understanding – discussion.

Section 2.4 emphasised the need for a clear knowledge of one's progress. Students who check their progress at regular intervals learn faster than those who plod on with no checks on what they have learnt. But an isolated student – at home, say – may find it difficult to check his progress. He may think he understands something which in reality he is still confused about. Discussion avoids this problem. You try explaining something you've just learnt to someone else. You're doing fine – and then he asks a question. Suddenly you don't know. You realise that, after all, you hadn't mastered the topic. Don't despair. You've just learnt something very important. You've learnt that you don't know something, or don't under-stand something, which previously you felt sure of. You have a clearer picture of your own progress. Through the discussion you have discovered which points you need to concentrate on in your next study session.

Discussion will also give you new ideas and new insights through listen-ing to someone else's ideas and experience. In fact the discussion process combines several functions:

(i) discussion tests your knowledge and understanding;

(ii) discussion brings you new ideas and insights;

(iii) discussion is an active reordering of the material in your mind.

You should, therefore, take every opportunity to discuss your subject with other people. They don't have to be experts although experts should by no means be avoided. But you can learn by talking over your subject with friends and family even when they have never studied the subject. Indeed, Mao is reputed to have said that the educator's job is to give the people in a clear and organised form what he has learnt from them in an unorganised form. So do try to tap your friends for ideas.

2.10 DEVELOPING LEARNING HABITS

'Successful studying, like successful dieting, calls not for sporadic bursts of good behaviour but for long-term adjustment to the pattern of one's daily habits' (*The Open University Study Guide* (1970) p. 6).

'. . . make a clean and determined break with all old habits which are detrimental to effective study'

R.B.JACKSON

Unless you have no need of this course, you should already be aware of discrepancies between good study habits and your own habits. How can you make the change?

Habits – good or bad – are, by definition, deeply rooted behaviour patterns. They are not changed easily. If you wish to study effectively, you must be prepared to make a clean and determined break with all old habits which are detrimental to effective study. This will not be easy.

First, list all those habits and activities which are hindering your study. Include bad study habits such as distracting activities like watching too much television. Now list all the good habits which you need to develop. Then resolve to make a clean break with the first list and to follow the second list without exception.

Sticking to your new behaviour pattern is very difficult at first. But stick to it you must if you wish this pattern to become a habit. There are various ways of reinforcing the new pattern. Try enlisting the help of your family. Tell them of your new intentions and ask them to remind you of any lapses. You can understand the effectiveness of this approach by considering the repentant smoker. A personal decision to give up smoking is hard to keep. Who will notice if you have 'just one more'? But, if you tell all your friends and family of your intention to stop smoking, every reach for a cigarette will be greeted with a chorus of reminders of your intention. So it is with study habits. Use your family or a friend as your conscience until the new behaviour pattern is an established routine – a habit.

2.11 CHECKLIST

You should now find that you have:
   (a) Made a list of things that distract you when you study and worked out how to reduce these distractions.
   (b) Made a list of things that you find easy to remember and a list of things that you find hard to remember. Analysed these lists to find out how to improve your memory techniques.
   (c) Found out what you are motivated to do and what you are not motivated to do. Developed some plans for improving your motivation.
   (d) Looked at the way in which you organise material and relate it to everyday life and developed some ideas for improving your techniques at these skills.

CHAPTER 3

READING

3.1 TYPES OF READING

Have you been reading this course at the same rate as you would read a novel or a page of a daily paper? If so, you have been reading it far too quickly unless you are having a quick preliminary read. You have ignored some of the points made in Chapter 2 on effective methods of study. There are many types of reading, each with its own purpose, each suited to a particular occasion.

The skilled reader is one who varies his reading speed and method to suit both the material he is reading and his reason for reading it.

If you are looking through a list of exam results to find your own result, you scan the list very quickly for your name. Having found your name, you will read the result against it very carefully – you'll probably read it several times just to make sure that you haven't made a mistake. This illustrates very clearly how you can vary your type of reading according to your purpose. Scanning for some vital point (your name); detailed, slow, attention to extract the crucial detail (your result).

As a student determined to study effectively and efficiently, you should try to cultivate a varied approach to reading. Here are some of the types of reading which you will need.

(a) Scanning

Scanning is a very rapid search for some important point. It may be a page number, a title or a key word. The essential point is that you deliberately ignore everything but the one item for which you are scanning. Some people are very bad at this because they refuse to try and concentrate. They let their attention wander and they start reading 'interesting' paragraphs, entirely forgetting their original purpose. A good student will need to become a good scanner. He may have to scan books or notes for a point for an essay. He may have to scan periodicals and indexes for items which might be important to his studies. A bad scanner is simply someone who allows his attention to be caught by matters which are irrelevant to the purpose in hand. If you find that your scanning is poor, turn back to section 2.1, 'Attention and interest', and try to apply the advice of that section to your scanning.

(b) Skimming

Skimming is very much like scanning except that you are not looking for anything in particular. You are simply looking to see what's there. For example you might pick up a book on Democracy and skim through it, looking at main ideas in the paragraphs, looking at chapter headings and so on, just to see whether or not the book interests you or is likely to be useful to you. If you were scanning the book, you might be looking to see if there were any section on, say, the birth of democracy in England. Everything else would be ignored in your search. Thus when you scan you are searching for something specific. But when you skim, you are assessing overall picture of the book or article.

(c) Reading to study

This is perhaps the type of reading which we normally associate with study. It is slow and repetitive. The aim is to master what is being read. At the end of reading one chapter in this manner, you will hope to have absorbed all the major facts, ideas and arguments in that chapter. Reading to study may well involve several readings and the taking of notes to summarise what has been read. Reading to study is dealt with in detail in Section 3.4:SQ3R.

(d) Light reading

This is the way most people read most of the time. Many novels are read like this - indeed the bulk of popular fiction deserves no more attention. Often the aim is escapism, to fly for an hour or two into another world, away from the problems and distress of the world of today. There is no attempt to digest the material. Nor is there any attempt to assess it critically. Such reading tends to be fast and superficial.

In its place, light reading is of great value. Through it much happiness and relief is created and it may save untold numbers from nervous breakdown. But just because many novels and newspapers are read in this way we must not consider all novels and newspaper articles as suitable for such treatment. Tolstoy and Forster, *The Times* and the *Guardian* deserve - demand - far more studious treatment. They put forward ideas of great moment and they demand that you study, criticise and assess those ideas.

(e) Word-by-word reading

There are certain types of material that demand word-by-word reading. They only need to be mentioned so that you don't feel ashamed when you find that you need this technique. The two most important occasions for word-by-word reading are foreign languages and mathematical and scientific formulae.

The ability to 'read' a line of print depends on familiarity with the material. A reader automatically recognises common words and phrases without actually focusing his eyes on every word and letter. Thus you only need to glance at

a stitch in time saves nine

to know what it says, whereas one like

methoxyhaemoglobinaemia

takes a lot of looking at. Yet 'methoxyhaemoglobinaemia' contains only more letter than 'a stitch in time saves nine'.

Thus the eye has to stop and dissect unfamiliar words, whereas it can take in familiar phrases at a glance. Since most foreign words are unfamiliar to a new student of the language, a word-by-word reading will be required before words and phrases become familiar.

Mathematical and scientific formulae are much like a foreign language, except in one respect. Formulae are highly condensed methods of conveying information. The simple formula

$$H_2O$$

contains the statement 'that which is formed when two atoms of hydrogen are combined with one atom of oxygen'. Without formulae, scientists and mathematicians would be buried under words. You must, therefore, expect to greatly slow down your reading whenever you read a formula. Of course, familiarity with a subject leads to familiarity with basic formula patterns. Thus

$$x = \frac{-b \pm \sqrt{b^2 - 4ac}}{2a}$$

is instantly recognised by all mathematicians, but for an 'O' level student, it represents quite a feat of understanding.

● **Activity 1 Choosing a reading method** ●

Which of the five methods of reading would you choose for the following:

  (i) Looking at a book in a bookshop to decide whether or not to buy it.

  (ii) Translating a foreign phrase.

28

(iii) Finding the symptoms and treatment of chicken-pox in a child-care book.
(iv) Studying Shakespeare for 'A' level.
(v) Reading a detective story.
(vi) Studying this book.
(vii) Checking your horoscope.
(viii) Looking in a book in a library to answer a specific query.
(ix) Reading the instructions for mixing a poisonous garden spray.

Your answers will vary since there can be several valid ways of approaching a reading task. My answers would be:
(i) Skimming with possibly some scanning.
(ii) Word by word.
(iii) Scanning (to find entry) followed by reading to study.
(iv) Reading for study and word by word.
(v) Light reading.
(vi) Reading for study.
(vii) Scanning (to find entry) followed by reading to study or word by word.
(viii) Scanning.
(ix) Word by word.

Summary

To study efficiently you must learn to vary your reading speed to suit both the material in front of you and your reason for reading that material. You must first aim at mastering each type of reading in your studies and in leisure reading. By developing the ability to flick from one method of reading to another you will vastly increase your efficiency. You will be able to search for specific items by scanning, to quickly assess a passage by skimming, to analyse and master a passage by studious reading. Nor should your lighter reading be neglected. Here too you can increase your efficiency by learning to read light or familiar material at a much faster speed than your present reading. The next section discusses ways of improving your reading skills.

• Activity 2 How you read now •

List all the reading you have done in the last seven days – including newspapers, advertisements etc. Now put 1, 2, 3, 4 or 5 against each item according to the reading method you used when you first read each item. Did you always use the most appropriate method?

3.2 HAVE YOU A READING SPEED PROBLEM?

(a) Your reading speed
You may have read of people who have reading speeds of 2000 words per minute. It was, for example, said that President Kennedy could read *Gone with the Wind* before breakfast. If that makes you feel out of it, don't worry. I know of no person who can read at such speeds - even though I know of plenty of able and intelligent people. I expect the people I know read most material at between 300 and 450 words per minute - slower for some things, a little faster for others. So if you usually read at a speed of around 300 words per minute you have no problem. But if your speeds are well below this, you could do with some practice. But first, what speed do you read at?

● **Activity 3 Check your reading speed** ●

Instructions
The following is an extract from the *Guardian* newspaper. Have ready some paper, a pen and a watch that can measure seconds. You are going to time yourself on reading this passage and then answer some questions to see if you have understood it. *If you really want to know how well you read you must read this passage at the speed you normally read a newspaper.*
    You start the exercise by noting the time. Start when you are ready to do this.

Time now　　　☐

Read this passage.

(739 words)

Time now　☐

Number of seconds to read　☐

Time out and wasted time
The TUC is pressing ahead with its plans for a politically motivated one-day general strike on May 14. That strike is designed to focus opposition to the Government's economic, social and industrial relations policies and to draw attention to the TUC's alternatives. The strike will undoubtedly be successful inasmuch as newspapers, public transport and much of industry will be disrupted. Whether it will tell the public anything that it does not

already know about the impact of Thatcherism or the implications of the TUC's more nebulous proposals is open to doubt. So, too, is the suggestion that the General Council call represents the considered judgment of the TUC's 12 million members. It is worth remembering that Mrs Thatcher is in office today because many millions of trade unionists voted for the Conservative party last May. Some will now be regretting the fact. (So, according to the polls, are many non-unionists.) But there must still be several million Conservative supporters in the ranks of the TUC. They merit some consideration from the General Council.

So, too, do those trade union critics of the Government who have grave reservations about both the relevance and the implications of the TUC's token stoppage. This week the executive of the Electrical, Electronic, Telecommunication and Plumbing Union, the sixth largest union in the TUC, gave voice to those reservations. Dismissing the strike call as 'untimely and unwise' the EETPU asked whether this was the proper way for unions to conduct themselves, particularly when, in the same month, many voters would have the opportunity of expressing their political views at the ballot box in local government elections. Further, the union asked what the 'Day of Action' (the TUC's chosen euphemism) really means. 'Is it intended to bring down the Government? If the Government does not change course as a result, will we have more Days of Action until they do?'

The Electricians warned the TUC that the token stoppage would do nothing to change government policies but would weaken support for the unions amongst both union members and the public. Finally the union drew attention to what it sees as the 'serious danger' that May 14 would push the TUC closer to an all-out general strike in the classical revolutionary sense. It is easy to smile at such hyperbole – especially when it comes from a union which has long been the odd man out around the Congress House council table and which is preoccupied (for internal, historic reasons) with Communist subversion. Of course the TUC is not planning to pull the Government down – either on May 14 or in the forseeable future. Mr Len Murray, in common sense mood, got it about right when he commented recently: 'I do not think the British people would tolerate that for one moment. If we did that we would not know what to do with the power we had got.' That was the lesson the TUC learned in 1926 and there is no evidence whatsoever that anybody of significance on the General Council wants a repeat performance. Folk memories are long in the trade union movement.

The serious accusation to be made against the TUC's Day of Action is not that it is the first step on the slippery slope to subversion. It is merely that such stoppages are very, very silly. For decades continental union federations have called token political strikes. Democracy survives without difficulty. So do the governments which have to endure them – and so, indeed, do their policies by and large. Until recently the General Council looked on these excesses with an indulgent smile. They were the actions of younger, weaker and less experienced organisations than our own TUC. Now Mr Murray and his colleagues wish to emulate their continental counterparts. But while Mr Murray has made it commendably clear that he is not in the business of political subversion, he has failed to answer the EETPU question about the purpose of May 14.

Does the General Council really believe that mass action is the right way to change government policies? Or that a one day strike will educate and inform the public – rather than aggravating and annoying them? And has it even begun to calculate the consequences – and the demands which will then rain in upon it – if the Government's response to the Day of Action is simply to turn a blind eye?

*(Guardian, 17 April 1980)

Now answer these questions. In each case only one of the options is correct.

1. The TUC strike was to be held (a) next day (b) 1 May (c) 14 May (d) 31 May.
2. In the author's view the strike would be successful because it would (a) disrupt the country (b) make people better informed about the Government's policy (c) persuade the Government to change its policy (d) get more members for the TUC.
3. The EETPU (a) is against the strike (b) is against calling the strike 'a day of action' (c) thinks the strike would bring the Government down (d) would prefer a general strike.
4. The TUC believes (a) the general public would support a general strike (b) it should try to bring the Government down (c) this should be the first of many days of action (d) the TUC view is not stated in the article.
5. The author believes that the Day of Action will (a) subvert democracy (b) help to bring British unions in line with continental unions (c) strengthen democracy (d) make the unions look silly.

How well have you done? First check your reading speed and comprehension on page 87. Now you want a balance between speed and comprehension - it is no use being a very fast reader if you understand nothing of what you read. Nor are you going to get far with perfect comprehension and a very low reading speed.

If you got four or five questions right then your comprehension is good. If you read the passage at a speed of 250 words per minute or more then your reading speed is good too. If either figure is lower, you would benefit from some practice using one of the many books on speed reading.

(b) How we read

When you meet a new and complex word, particularly a foreign word, you stop and read each letter in turn. Then you try and build the letters into pronounceable syllables. But this is not the normal method of reading. A quick reader looks at perhaps four points on a line of print and in those four glances he reads the whole line. Whether you are a good or bad reader, you can probably take in

a pound of sugar

at a glance. But you may look several times at

an aptitude for spacial visualisation.

Now there is no shame in finding the second phrase more difficult to comprehend than the first. In the first phrase, not only the words, but the particular combination of words, are a familiar part of everyday speech. But the second phrase uses uncommon words in an uncommon construction. Only those few people who indulge in a study of human perception would be familiar with such a phrase.

That is the ideal situation. Unfortunately many readers are so inefficient that they have to look at phrases like 'a pound of sugar' more than once to take them in. Faced with a simple sentence like

John has just been round the corner to buy a pound of sugar.

they make an excessive number of eye fixations on the page and at the same time they keep backtracking. A good reader might make these fixations:

1   2

John has just been round the corner to buy a pound of sugar.

A slow reader might read thus:

     1   2   3   4   5   6   7
John has just been round the corner to buy a pound of sugar.

But a poor reader will not only make too many fixations, he will also backtrack.

     2   1   3   4   6 5   7 8 10 9 11
John has just been round the corner to buy a pound of sugar.

The eye fixation 2, 6 and 10 are on items which have already been read. They should, therefore, be completely unnecessary.

    Thus, if you are a slow reader (200 wpm or below), you will have all or some of the following faults:

> **Poor reading summary**
> 1. Failure to adjust reading speed to material.
> 2. Mouthing the words (sub vocalisation).
> 3. Low vocabulary – too many words are unfamiliar.
> 4. Too many eye fixations.
> 5. Regressive eye fixations (backtracking).
> 6. The cause may be poor eyesight – see an optician.

   ● **Activity 4 Check your faults** ●
Have you any of these reading faults?
List them now before reading the section on correcting reading faults.

(c) Correcting reading faults

You may well have seen advertisements for commercial speed-reading courses. They claim to offer you reading speeds of not hundreds, but thousands, of words per minute. Maybe many people have passed through their courses and found them satisfactory, but two important points should be remembered.

    (i) All 'better reading' courses seem to produce the same average result. The students start at around 250 wpm and end at around 500 wpm.

    (ii) For any individual to exceed 600 wpm is very rare and such a speed should not be considered as a general aim for all students. Experience has shown that the average reader can produce just as great an improvement in his reading speed and comprehension through following a 'better reading' book, as he can through an expensive course with lectures, films and so on.

'The cause may be poor eyesight – see an optician'

The best book is *Read Better, Read Faster.* Provided you follow the authors' instructions, you should quickly achieve a significant improvement in your reading.

Even without a full course it should be possible to make a start on correcting some of your poor reading habits. Here are some hints for overcoming the poor habits listed at the end of the last section.

(i) Failure to adjust reading speed

Practise reading very light material as fast as you can, forcing yourself to read forward all the time without back-tracking. Newspapers are ideal for this purpose, since much of their content is light and the narrow columns encourage you to read a line at a glance. Regular practice at this type of exercise should produce an increase in light reading speed within two to four weeks. You should have no difficulty in slowing down for more serious study. Try to do a little of each type of reading each day. Make a conscious effort to keep a fast pace all through the light piece and a slow, studious, pace through the other piece.

(ii) Mouthing words

Readers who silently mouth the words can never hope to read much faster than they speak until they break this habit. The only way out is to practise reading very much faster than you can speak. Thus, following the instructions in (i) should help break this habit. Some authorities recommend reading a passage and reciting numbers or the alphabet aloud. This certainly prevents the vocal chords from mouthing the words you read, but it is rather difficult to keep up.

(iii) Low vocabulary

The whole of the next subsection is devoted to extending your vocabulary, so it will not be discussed here.

(iv) Too many eye fixations

In a normal line of print with material which is reasonably easy to comprehend, three or four eye fixations should prove sufficient to read the line. Practise deliberately fixing your eye on specific points of the page as you read and try to see all the words from these points, thus:

1	2	3	4
1	2	3	4
1	2	3	4

(v) Regressive eye fixations

These can be cured both by practising fast reading as in (i) and by using definite fixation points as in (iv). Whenever you are practising your reading, keep your eyes moving across the page. Concentrate on forcing them along the line, avoiding the temptation to backtrack.

You will find that as little as 10 minutes daily practice will produce a very significant improvement in your reading skills within three to four weeks. Kept up for six weeks, such practice will eradicate almost every trace of your poor reading habits.

● **Activity 5 A plan for improvement** ●
If you are a slow reader start correcting your faults now. Get a newspaper and do ten minutes' practice at faster reading.

3.3 EXTENDING YOUR VOCABULARY

● **Activity 6 Try your vocabulary** ●
Here are ten words I have used in this course. For each word, write down a sentence of your own incorporating that word. Then check the meaning of the word in a dictionary.

1. relevant
2. artificial
3. incessant
4. controversial
5. cliché
6. proposition
7. apt
8. counteract
9. consistent
10. ensure

If you found that easy, then you haven't any vocabulary problems worth bothering about. But what if you had some problems?

When it comes to study, one of the commonest difficulties is lack of familiarity with the language used by the authors you read. The normal vocabulary of everyday gossip gets by on 2000-3000 words. The average person has a latent (i.e. total words he knows, whether or not he uses them) vocabulary of 20,000-25,000 words whereas his active vocabulary is nearer the 3000 word gossip level. But for study, an active vocabulary of something like 25,000 words is needed. How can you bridge the gap?

Extending one's vocabulary is quite easy and is nothing like learning the lists of words which teachers used to be so fond of. The lists of difficult words printed in popular magazines do not, as claimed, improve your vocabulary. The mere learning of words and their meanings quickly fades from memory and as fast as you take in new words you are losing words learnt two or three weeks ago. No, successful vocabularly extension relies on applying your knowledge of memory and learning (see Section 2.5). You will remember that material which is understood, is linked with previous knowledge and is applied in everyday life, is mastered and memorised more quickly than material which is learnt by rote. The following guides to a better vocabulary are all based on this simple principle.

(a) Read widely

Almost all the words you know were learnt in context. That is, as a child, you heard others use the words over and over again in many different contexts, and so you learnt the meaning of the word. Any other method of learning would be impossibly complex for a child. Imagine trying to define 'pretty' to a five-year-old! Yet most five-year-olds use the word without the slightest difficulty. They do this because they have an intuitive understanding of what 'pretty' means from the various occasions on which it has been used by others.

Similarly the best way in which an adult can broaden his vocabulary is by reading widely so as to meet new words in a variety of contexts. It is, of course, no use just doing a lot of reading in one field. A diet of novels or biology or horror stories will not do. You would not meet enough new words in a sufficient range of contexts to clearly establish them in your own vocabulary.

(b) Use new words

Some new words will find their way into your vocabulary without any conscious effort. But you can also gain something by deliberately using new words as you meet them. It may help to list those words which you feel are of particular importance – e.g. those which you will need for your studies. You can then look at the list and determine to use some of the words in the near future.

(c) Look up words

On the whole, we learn very few words through consulting dictionaries. But occasionally you will meet a word without being able to grasp its meaning from the context. When this happens, look up the word in a dictionary and make a note of its meaning. You can go over such lists from time to time, but don't try to commit them verbatim to memory. You may find it useful to have *Roget's Thesaurus* to hand. This book has been continuously in print since 1852 which is measure enough of its value. Words are grouped under topics. For example, entry 705 in the Penguin edition is 'opponent'. The entry reads:

705. Opponent – N. opponent, opposer, lion in the path; adversary, antagonist 881 n. enemy; assailant 712 n. attacker; the opposition, ranks of Tuscany, opposite camp; oppositionist, radical; obstructionist, filibuster 702 n. hinderer; cross-benches; die-hard, irreconcilable; radical of the right, reactionary; objector 489 n. dissentient; non-cooperator 829 n. malcontent; agitator 738 n. revolter; challenger, other candidate, rival, emulator, competitor, entrant, the field, all comers 716 n. contender.

All the words are listed in an alphabetical index to the *Thesaurus* which quickly guides you to words and phrases suitable to a particular context. The Penguin edition of the *Thesaurus* is very good value for money. If you prefer a hardback edition, but don't want to pay a lot, look in second-hand bookshops.

(d) Other techniques
There are also several painless ways of extending your vocabulary. For example, games like Scrabble or completing a daily crossword puzzle.

● **Activity 7 Use your dictionary** ●
Find five words in this course which you don't understand.
Check their meaning in the dictionary.
Make this a habit for new words that you come across in the future.

3.4 SQ3R

This is not a mathematic formula, not a mysterious code. SQ3R simply stands for:

S	Survey
Q	Question
R	Read
R	Recall
R	Review

It is a useful method of approaching a passage, such as a chapter of a book, which you want to study and master. The idea is that your reading of the passage is broken down into five stages. The details of each stage are explained below.

(a) Survey
This is rather like the skimming process which you met in 3.1. To survey a book you look at the following items:

title
author
date of first publication and date of this edition
preface and introduction
contents page
chapter headings
index

The survey stage gives you a general impression of the type of book you are reading. If you are going to concentrate on one chapter, the survey stage ensures that you also have an adequate impression of the book as a whole. The date of publication ensures that you have an idea of the historical context in which the book was written. Obviously you will approach a book on chemistry written in 1850 in a very different way from a chemistry book of 1980.

Reading the preface and introduction ensures that you understand the author's proposed intention in writing the book. He may explain why he has taken a particular line, why he has omitted certain items and so on.

Looking at the index acts as a guide to the type of notes you might wish to make. A poorly indexed book, or one with no index at all, requires better note-taking than a well-indexed book.

(b) Question

Before embarking on the book or chapter, ask yourself what you expect to gain from the book. Why are you reading the book? What points are you particularly interested in? These sort of questions ensure that you read with a purpose.

You might even ask 'Is the book worth reading?' To answer this, read its first and last paragraphs then its first and last chapters. This should help you decide whether it is worth studying.

(c) Read

In the case of one chapter, you will find it best to read it at least twice at a fair speed before you study it in detail. You will be looking for the author's general stance for this chapter and also for the basic idea in each paragraph. Then you will look at the detail. What evidence does the author produce to back up his argument? Look at his examples, his proofs. Can you think of any contrary examples? Is there a flaw in his proof?

Look at the diagrams and illustrations. What purpose does the author have in choosing these diagrams and illustrations? What points do they illustrate?

Then look at the author's case in the round. Is the chapter convincing? Are there alternative theories which would do just as well in the circumstances? What consequences flow from the author's theory? What consequences flow from your alternative theories?

You will notice that at the beginning of the read stage, you are simply trying to grasp what the author says. You are trying to understand his arguments. Only when you completely follow the author's case do you turn to criticising it. If you criticise too soon you will fail to listen to what the author has to say and be carried away by your own ideas.

(d) Recall

This stage may follow the read stage for the whole chapter, or, if the chapter is rather lengthy or complex, it may follow the read stage for sections of the chapter.

The recall stage involves trying to recall all the main ideas in the section under recall. It is best either to recite them aloud or to write them down in note form.

(e) Review

The review stage is the checking which follows recall. Look back over the chapter and check that your recall was correct. Make a special note of any important points which you failed to recall, or which you wrongly recalled.

> ● **Activity 8 Using SQ3R** ●
> Take a book you are studying or any other book that interests you and demands working at in order to be understood. Apply the SQ3R method to one chapter as follows:
>
> 1. Survey it in 2 minutes, jotting down what you observe.
> 2. Now note down the questions you hope to be able to answer by reading it. Allow 2-5 minutes for this.
> 3. Read.
> 4. Close the book. Jot down the main points of the chapter.
> 5. Review what you jotted down in (4) against your questions in (2) and the chapter itself.

If you have taken this activity seriously then there is a very good chance that you understand that chapter better than almost anything else you have studied. It is a powerful method - try to use it regularly.

3.5 CHOOSING BOOKS

If you are following a set course of study, there will almost certainly be a few books which are compulsory reading. In addition to these, there will probably be a recommended book list. It is very unlikely that you will have time to study more than a small section from the list, so choosing the books must be done with care.

But which books do you need for which purpose? If you have been thinking about the applications of skimming, scanning, SQ3R and so on, you will be aware that we can use books in many different ways. Some study books are read intensively from cover to cover. This is the case with a textbook when the whole of your course is based on it. Other books are used for reference on a regular basis, e.g. a dictionary or a book of grammar. Still others are used for occasional reference, perhaps to answer one problem only. Others are used for short periods whilst you work on a topic, as you might do in a project.

With all these different ways of using books, it doesn't make sense for you to obtain all your books in the same way. Some you need to buy because you need them for a long period of intensive use. Others you need to buy because you need them occasionally but regularly, e.g. a dictionary. Others are best borrowed.

● **Activity 9 How do you choose books?** ●
Look at the books that you currently have to hand for your study. Classify them as follows:

Title   Own/borrowed   Use I make of it

Does this show that your system of organising your access to books works well for you or not?

3.6 CHECKLIST

You should now find that you have:
(a) learnt to distinguish the various types of reading and practised their use:
(b) checked your reading and comprehension speeds;
(c) established whether you have any reading faults;
(d) checked whether you have any problems with vocabulary;
(e) practised the SQ3R method of studying a book;
(f) looked at your use of books.

CHAPTER 4

OTHER LEARNING TECHNIQUES

4.1 NOTE-TAKING

(a) Why keep notes?

The primary purpose of notes is to aid memory. Whether the notes are taken from a lecture, a book or a discussion, you can't hope to permanently retain the whole lecture, book or discussion in your memory. Instead you make notes of the most important items and use the notes for revision and reference. The items selected for inclusion in the notes are sufficient for you to be able to reconstruct the rest of the material.

But notes which are a pure summary of what was said or written may not mean much to you. The importance of reordering and reorganising study material has already been stressed in Section 2.2, 'Memory', and Section 2.5, 'Learning'. The making of notes is one of the most important occasions for rearranging material in whichever form is most useful to you. For many types of course there are printed notes sold by booksellers. These are quite useless since they are not arranged to suit you. You might as well memorise the original lecture or book as memorise printed notes.

A third purpose behind note-taking is that the acutal process aids concentration and promotes learning. Making notes on a particular passage requires more concentration and effort than does plain reading. Active methods of learning such as recitation and writing promote learning and hold the concentration far better than passive methods such as reading and thinking – so much so that many children cannot learn to read simply through the use of the usual printed readers and cards. Such children have to feel the shape of letters and words by cutting them out of sandpaper or tracing them in sand. These 'kinaesthetic' methods are just as useful to adults; you will find the use of physical activity essential to efficient study.

Of course the overall purpose of your notes is to gain success in your studies. It is helpful to bear this in mind when deciding what to include in your notes and how to arrange them. Notes which do not help towards this long-term aim should be discarded.

● **Activity 1 Looking at your notes** ●

Try to find several different sets of notes which you have previously made. For each set, try to answer the following questions:

What are these notes about?

What did I make them for?

How well did they serve that purpose?

Does this activity tell you anything about how good your note-making skills are already?

(b) Characteristics of good notes

There are no hard and fast rules here, simply because notes are such a personal learning and memory aid. On the whole, though, the following general observations apply to most types of notes.

Notes should be brief and clear. If they are too long, it will be a tedious job to wade through them, either to look for a specific point, or to refresh your memory. Once made, your notes are your primary source of information and, if you are to take an exam, you will be aiming at complete familiarity with their contents. You should, at the outset, create notes which you can understand. If the notes are such that you cannot quickly read through them to refresh your memory, they will fail in their purpose.

● **Activity 2 Another look at your notes** ●

For each of the sets of notes which you used in Activity 1 check which of these characteristics they had.

Easily read	☐	Difficult to read	☐
Brief	☐	Long	☐
Clear	☐	Unclear	☐
Easily understood	☐	Difficult to understand	☐
Organised the way *I* learn	☐	Organised in some other way	☐
Relevant to my needs	☐	Not relevant to my needs	☐

Have you given yourself lots of ticks in the left-hand column? If you have then you have an excellent note-making system. But if you have lots of ticks in the right-hand column then you need a new approach to note-making.

(c) Types of notes

There are two types of notes: sequential and nuclear. The chances are that you have only met sequential notes. These look like Figure 4.1. But you can also make nuclear notes on the same topic as in Figure 4.2. However, before you make any notes you need to describe why you are making them. Basically you will be in one of two situations. Either you will be hurriedly making notes to capture something that is only briefly available.

This would be the case when making notes during a lecture. Or you will be making notes in your own time which gives you much more opportunity to rearrange material to suit you and your purpose.

Notes made under pressure (as in a lecture) are therefore only temporary, being kept only until you have time to make better organised notes. I will now look at these different situations in more detail.

Fig 4.1   *sequential notes*

Attention
Depends on   interest
                      removing other stimuli
                      understanding
                      taking a lively interest

Memory
The learning curve

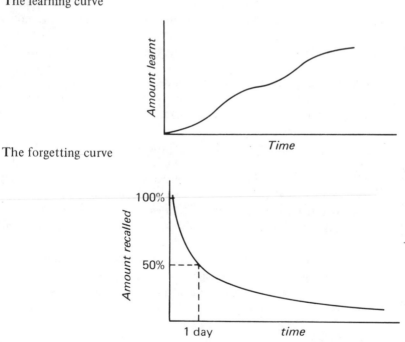

The forgetting curve

Things which are easy to remember
                  Things with a pattern
                  Logical things
                  Unusual things

Fig 4.2 *nuclear notes*

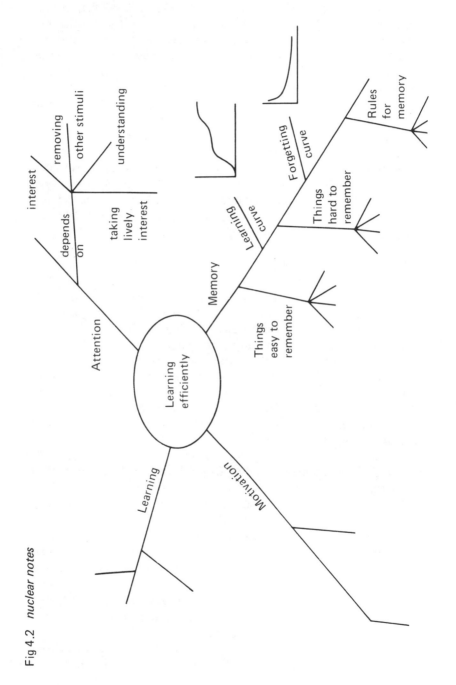

(i) Notes from lectures

Note-taking from lectures and broadcasts requires more skill than note-taking from books. With the book you can always go back and check a point, but a lecture or broadcast goes on relentlessly. This factor may necessitate making fuller notes so that you can select and reorganise the material at a later stage. To what extent you can make usable notes at the time depends on the style of the speaker. Some ramble on, backtrack, lose their way, until no one knows exactly what stage has been reached. With such a lecturer, it may be impossible to even extract the topic headings during the lecture. This, unfortunately, means that the student has a lot of extra work to do after the lecture. Where this is the case, remember the 'forgetting curve' in Section 2.2 – that is, go over your notes as soon as possible after the lecture before the detail fades from memory. With good lecturers, on the other hand, it should be possible to follow the lecturer's own logical subdivision of his lecture, and so make more intelligible notes during the lecture.

(ii) Making notes from books

You should not start to make summary notes on a book until you have read the relevant parts of the book by the SQ3R method (Section 3.4). This method ensures that you understand what you have read and, naturally, you should not make notes on things you don't understand. During the SQ3R process you will have already made a summary of the main points and, possibly, a note of the main point in each paragraph. Now these notes were made in order to understand what the author was trying to say. Consequently they are not necessarily in a suitable form for permanent notes. In making permanent notes you will want to do your own rearranging of the material and, possibly, you will want to add your own comments and cross-references to other notes.

Although you may be aiming to summarise what is said in a particular book or chapter, you are not aiming to précis that book or chapter. Thus your notes will be in your own words and phrases, not the author's. (There will be a few occasions where you may need to record a direct quotation, but these will be an exception). The process of converting the ideas into your own language ensures that you understand the material. If you cannot restate the ideas clearly, then it is likely that you haven't understood them.

You should try to record the main topics covered and then the important points under each topic. These will tend to be headings or brief statements. Where an argument, proof or deductive process is presented, try to note down the main steps, but don't pare the argument down so much that you can't restate the missing processes.

Your notes should also record the major conclusions, results and so on of each chapter. Thus your framework might be something like this.

    Chapter heading (in your own words, maybe).
       Important points in chapter.
          Illustrations and arguments to support points.
          Results/conclusions of chapter.

Under no circumstances should you regard this as a skeleton outline for all notes, but it illustrates the type of thing you should be looking for when making notes.

Finally, don't forget to record the title and author of the book from which you've been working. You may need to quote it, or to come back to check a point.

(iii) Methods of laying out notes

Sequential notes. This is the commonest form of layout but, common as it is, it is an ill-understood form. Too often people's sequential notes are just pages and pages of what someone else has said or what someone else has written. If you have ever tried to learn or revise from such notes, you will know how ineffective they are.

If sequential notes are to be of any use to you then they must reinforce all that you have learnt about memory and understanding in Chapter 2. The material in the notes must be in your own words, it must be related to previous knowledge, it must have pattern. You need to use as many aids as possible to put the material into a form which immediately promotes understanding. This will mean using diagrams, tables, lists, memory aids and so on. In fact, so important is this personal rearranging of material for notes that your notes will probably be almost useless to someone else.

Nuclear notes. These go part of the way towards organising the information just by the way they are made. You start by writing the name of the topic in the centre of the page. Then you add a branch for each main idea and then you subdivide the branches, subdivided again if you want, and so on . . . Some people even start adding links around the edge where these seem to be needed. The result is something like Figure 4.2.

Before I go any further, you ought to try both methods and see what you think of them.

       ● **Activity 3 Sequential and nuclear notes** ●
      Make notes on Chapter 3, first in sequential form and then in nuclear form.

Which method is best? I doubt that there is an answer to this and I certainly don't intend to give one. In any case, the question, as with all study skills is, 'which is best for you?' But it is worth noting that some topics are easier to put into one format and some into the other. Nuclear notes make relationships very clear but are not so good where solid fact is important. Thus you could make notes on the causes of the World War I more easily in nuclear form that you could on the Atomic Table.

A second point which I think is useful to note is that nuclear notes can be very useful as halfway notes *helping* you sort something out. It is easier with nuclear notes to pop down an odd idea which you can't yet fit into your material. But later when you have worked out all the relationships, you may want to make your final notes in sequential form.

Finally, if you can't decide between the two, you can always use a mixture of both, e.g. one topic in nuclear form, another in linear, or basic notes in nuclear form with extra material on a facing sheet in linear form.

4.2 FILING

(a) Purposes

A pocket cartoon used to adorn the front of a filing cabinet in our office. A secretary, clutching a wadge of papers, was addressing her boss. 'Do you want this again, Sir, or shall I file it?'

Too many filing systems are like that. And the average person's ability to create a useful filing system is pretty low. The majority of people plump for the alphabetical system which, whilst simple, is not good on retrieval. Retrieval, however, is what it's all about. We create filing systems in order to take information out of them at a later date.

> ● **Activity 1 Purpose of filing systems** ●
> Look at the following filing systems. On what principles are they based and for what purpose were they created?
> > (i) Telephone directory
> > (ii) Street directory
> > (iii) Library subject index
> > (iv) Library author index

This activity emphasises that a filing system's design depends totally on what you are going to use it for. A telephone directory lists people in alphabetical order because we want to use it to find the telephone number of a person whose name we know. It would be no use trying to use the directory to find the name of a person whose number we knew. Much the same people will appear in a street directory but this is arranged by streets so it can only tell use who lives in a particular street and not where a given person lives. Finally the examples of two library indexes show how the same information can be organised in two different ways to serve two

'A filing system's design depends totally on what you are going to use it for'

different purposes. Titles of books can either be grouped according to the subject of the books (e.g. a group of books on gardening on acid soils) or we can list all the books by a given author. We need the first index when we want to find out what books there are on a topic. We need the second index when we want to find where the library have put a book by a particular author.

(b) Natural and artificial classification

There are two basic filing systems. The system of *artificial classification* groups material according to one characteristic only. For example, an artificial classification of people would be brought about by subdividing them into English speaking and non-English speaking. An artificial classification of animals might divide them into two-legged and other than two-legged. Artificial classifications are extremely sensitive to the single factor arbitrarily chosen for the classifying. As a result, artificial classification produces some odd results. The two-legged division of animals puts man and the sparrow in one division and cows and centipedes in another. Artificial schemes have their uses – nationality is an artificial classification.

On the other hand, *natural classifications* are more useful. In a natural classification we look for overall similarity. This leads us to divide people into men and women; dwellings into bungalows, houses, cottages, flats; living things into birds, mammals, plants etc. Although natural classifications are still somewhat arbitrary, they lead to a more stable division of the material than do artifical schemes.

(c) The alphabetical system (an artificial scheme)

The position of any item in an alphabetical system is determined purely by the accidents of language. A library which filed its books alphabetically would be very difficult to use. Books on Christmas and chrysanthemums would come close together but books on roses would be many shelves away. But as soon as the list of topics is more than can be read through in a minute or so, the alphabetical system becomes tedious.

As the amount of information you want to file grows, it might be useful to use a semi-alphabetical system. Here you would have a heading gardening and underneath that heading topics like roses would appear in alphabetical order.

Of course the alphabetical system is ideal for material which does not need to be grouped – names in a telephone directory. But if you were a postman you would group the same people by street, not by name. Thus in choosing a filing system you must bear in mind how and why you are going to retrieve information from it.

(d) Subject filing (a natural scheme)
Almost certainly you will wish to file the bulk of your notes by subject.
Headings for a biologist might include:
Cytology (the study of cells)
Ecology
Vertebrates
and so on.
Now it must be remembered that any filing system is arbitrary. Thus there
will always be awkward cases. Where, in the above system, do we file notes
on Vertebrate ecology? The answer is that you make a decision to file it
either under Ecology or under Vertebrates and then you insert a cross-
reference note under the other heading. Thus:
Cytology
Ecology. *See also* Vertebrate ecology
Vertebrates
    Vertebrate ecology
or
Cytology
Ecology
    Vertebrate ecology
Vertebrates. *See also* Vertebrate ecology *under* Ecology.

● **Activity 2 Creating a filing system** ●
Design a filing system for your notes on this book or on any other
course which you are following.
    Start by writing down the purpose to which you are going to put
the system. Only when that is absolutely clear in your mind will you
be able to design a good system to meet your requirements.

(e) Physical filing systems
Even when you have chosen a classification for your notes, you will
still need a physical interpretation of that scheme.

(i) Filing folders
One of the best schemes is the loose-leaf filing folder. It has many advan-
tages over other schemes.
    (i) New material can be inserted at any point.
    (ii) Material can be subdivided with commercially made, tabulated,
        divisions.
    (iii) The system can be endlessly expanded, if necessary beyond the
        original folder to a whole range of folders.
    (iv) Material can be reordered quickly.
To achieve the full advantage of a loose-leaf system you should only

write on one side of the paper and start new topics on new sheets of paper. Then any one topic can be removed or altered or reordered without upsetting other notes. Writing on one side only allows additions to be made opposite existing notes.

The loose-leaf system has so many advantages over the traditional notebook as to render the notebook obsolete.

Where a great physical variety of material is involved, the loose-leaf system may be inappropriate. For example, if you have notes, pamphlets, maps, diagrams, press-cuttings and so on, it may be difficult to ring-bind them all. In such circumstances, a series of large folders, designed for use in filing cabinets, will solve the problem.

Despite the incessant recommendation of the use of foolscap notepads and foolscap filing folders, you will be better off with an A4 pad. The 'A' sizes of paper are new international standards and leading organisations already use A4 as their standard paper. Because some foolscap is still in use, you may need a foolscap ring binder for filing both your A4 notes and other items on foolscap.

(ii) Card filing

Card filing is extremely useful for small items of information. Like the loose-leaf system, it is easily added to, amended, reordered and so on. In addition, it is easy to index the cards by a clear entry on the top left-hand corner. The standard size of card is 5 by 3 inches but for handwritten work the larger sizes are also useful: 6 by 4 inches and 8 by 5 inches.

4.3 CHECKLIST

You should now find that you have:
   (a) Examined and analysed your existing notes.
   (b) Worked out the characteristics of good notes.
   (c) Decided on when and where you can best use sequential notes and nuclear notes.
   (d) Decided on the best type of filing system for your study material.

CHAPTER 5

ESSAY WRITING

5.1 INTRODUCTION

If you can talk clearly and logically and interest your listeners, you should be able to do the same in writing. Writing is just a more permanent form of communicating your ideas. Provided you can really believe this, provided you can feel the truth of it, you should have no difficulty in writing effective essays.

A good essay is an interesting essay. If you have nothing of interest to say, no amount of style, presentation or juggling of words will repair your initial failing. The art of good essay writing lies in having something to say and saying it clearly and concisely.

In the 'real' world you have to write on a particular topic because it is necessary to do so. You either write what you have to say, or you don't. But in exams and tests you will normally find yourself with a choice of topic to write on. Choose a topic which you know and understand well, rather than something new and unfamiliar. If you have no choice and find yourself committed to an unfamiliar topic, read about that topic before you even begin to plan your essay or make notes for it. Should you fail to understand a topic before you write on it, you will be unable to select material for inclusion or develop a logical argument around the material you select.

5.2 LOOKING AT THE TITLE

Your starting point is your title or topic. Many is the student who has put hours of effort into his own interpretation of an allotted topic. The title is your marching orders. Follow them and you are well on the way to a good essay. Ignore tham and you will write an irrelevant essay. Here are some examples of related essay topics, each of which demands very different treatment from the others.

'Writing is just a more permanent form of communicating your ideas'

Describe the constitutional crisis which led to the Civil War.

Cromwell: democrat or dictator?

How could Charles I have saved his throne and head?

The first topic is largely descriptive, although it demands some interpretation of events. You would, for example, have to select those events which you consider brought about the crisis and reject other coincidental occurrences. Superficially the other two titles relate to the same events. But one concentrates on Cromwell and the other on Charles I. Note also that the most controversial part of Cromwell's life follows the death of Charles I. Thus the second two topics cover differing periods of history. Another point to note is that the first topic is largely descriptive; the second asks you to interpret events; the third asks you to imagine alternative events. For many students the danger is to see all three titles as one topic: the Civil War. As a result they pour out their textbook knowledge of the events of the Civil War and neglect the special emphasis of the essay title.

● **Activity 1 What the title asks for** ●

Here are three essay titles followed by nine items which might or might not be relevant to the titles. Which items are relevant to which titles and which are irrelevant?

Titles

(i) Do modern farming methods damage the environment?

(ii) Should politics be kept out of sport?

(iii) Motor cars are more a curse than a blessing.

Items

(a) What we mean by something being political.

(b) Accident figures on roads.

(c) Effects of hedgerows and trees on climate and soil.

(d) Information on how to service a motor car.

(e) Effects of sporting boycotts.

(f) The social changes resulting from our being a more mobile nation than in the past.

(g) An account of why you distrust politicians.

(h) A discussion of the morality of eating meat.

(i) The costs of different methods of farming.

There are no absolutely right answers to Activity 1 - with sufficiently ingenious arguments, almost any item of information can be shown to have some relationship to any other item. But most students who have trouble in writing essays introduce information which they are not able to relate to the title. They put the information down because they know it and not because they know how to use it. Students at this stage of developing essay-writing skills should stick to using clearly relevant material. On that basis, my answers to the activity would be:

(c) is relevant to (i)

(a) and (e) are relevant to (ii)

(b) and (f) are relevant to (iii)

5.3 GATHERING YOUR MATERIAL

Having a topic before you adds interest and purpose to study so it is sometimes useful to keep essay titles in mind from the beginning of a lesson or book. Knowing the topic on hand you can start gathering notes and ideas. At 'A' level and beyond this may involve reading books, extracting pieces from your notes, checking points in books which don't require a full reading. Quite often this is the most difficult and time-consuming part of essay writing. However good your knowledge of the topic, you will still have to devote a lot of thought to how you are going to treat the topic. What material will be included? What rejected? Which ideas are worth pursuing? Which theories are worth developing? Because of this difficulty, it is unwise to try and work solidly at this stage. It is better to work for a few hours and then leave the topic for a day or two. Meanwhile your mind will continue to work on the subject and you will find new ideas developing all the time.

● **Activity 2 Collecting relevant material** ●

Using the essay titles in Activity 1, write down five items of material that you would want to include in an essay on each title.

5.4 PLANNING THE OUTLINE

To some extent planning an outline for your essay is bound up with gathering your material. You will be developing an outline as you go along. But only when you feel you have all the material you need should you write down the outline in a firm and committed manner.

The first limitation on your outline is length. Given a limit of 2000 words you will have to be far more selective than for 5000 words. Make sure that you take this into account at the outline stage. If you don't, you will have to replan when the essay is half written.

An outline is a series of headings with perhaps an odd idea of two under each heading. But basically it is just the headings. The outline headings should do no more than cover the points you intend to write about. Logical order is the priority in the outline. This does not mean that there is one and only one order which you can consider. But it does mean that your final order must justify itself and be seen to do so by the reader.

In choosing an order, it is useful to consider the interest of the reader. Journalists carry this to extreme lengths so that their main idea is always in the first sentence. Not a good rule for essay writing, but there is a lesson there in how to catch your reader.

It is at the outline stage that you are going to have to be most selective. The headings you use will determine the material covered, the detail you go into, the number of theories considered and the number of examples quoted. To a great extent, the art of effectively presenting an argument lies in the selection process.

Once again, it is difficult to prepare an outline in a few hours. It is better to draft an outline and leave it for a day or two and then come back with new ideas. At this stage you can make a final outline which you will only adjust if the experience of writing the essay demands it.

● **Activity 3 Looking at essay outlines** ●
Here are two outlines for an essay on 'Should we keep our comprehensive schools?' Which do you think is better and why?

Outline (i)
What is a comprehensive school?
Are the schools which we call comprehensive proper comprehensives?
Initial conclusion on how far we have a comprehensive system at all?
Why did the people in favour of comprehensives want them in the first place? What benefits were they looking for? What ills were they trying to eliminate?
Evidence for success or failure in achieving these goals.
What reasons might there be/are given for changing what we have now?
Likely consequences of a change.
Conclusion.

Outline (ii)
Grammar schools were good schools so we should have kept them.
Big schools don't work.
Exam results are bad in comprehensives.
People should be able to choose the kind of school they want.
Conclusion.

You probably didn't have much trouble in identifying (i) as the better outline. Are your reasons the same as mine?

Outline (ii) takes bits and pieces of comment that are made about comprehensive and grammar schools but it doesn't look as though it is going to be able to make a coherent argument out of them. Outline (i) on the other hand tackles the topic systematically and probes the meaning of the terms being used. It asks questions even about the meaning of the title, which appears to ask a simple question that on close inspection is actually very complicated.

Outline (i) also shows that it is going to consider the evidence for and against and to test claims with evidence. It is not just going to make black and white statements.

The point of this activity is to emphasise that even at the level of a short outline, a good essay is beginning to stand out from a bad one. What this activity cannot show is how much more efficient it is to make sure that you have your outline well worked out before you start writing. It saves a lot of bother.

That happened with this book – and writing a book is no different in principle from writing an essay. I wrote an eight-page outline that showed the chapters, the chapter sections and all the activities. I then discussed it with the editor and we made several changes - cutting out some sections, putting others in. Now if I hadn't worked the outline out in a clear form, the editor might not have spotted the changes he thought advisable until I had finished the book. So I would have had to make big changes at the end instead of small changes at the beginning. The moral is that the little extra effort needed to produce a good outline is well repaid through preventing wasted effort later on.

So, if outlines are so important, a little practice will also prove well worthwhile.

● **Activity 4 Essay outlines** ●
Sketch out outlines for essay on the three titles in Activity 1.

5.5 WRITING THE ESSAY

Everyone worries about style when writing. Good style involves saying what you want to say clearly and concisely. Pompous language, excessively long or complex sentences, hackneyed phrases, clichés are to be rejected.

To be ruthless is difficult. We are surrounded by pompous English which is frequently encouraged by officials as good English.

Consider the policeman:

> 'I was proceeding down the High Street when I apprehended the said defendant in the act of purloining a motor vehicle on the Queen's Highway.'

All he means is that he saw Mr Jones stealing a car in the High Street.

Or the business man (cited by Sir Ernest Gowers in his *Complete Plain Words*):

'The non-compensable evaluation heretofore assigned to you for your service-connected disability is confirmed and continued.'

(What he means is anyone's guess.)

Improving your style is not so much a question of textbooks or exercises as it is of wide reading. Note the tendency of less able thinkers to wrap up a poor argument in verbose phrases and rambling paragraphs.

Of course there are occasions when jargon is necessary to convey a precise meaning. The social sciences require jargon to avoid the looser type of thinking which we use in everyday life. But on the whole, simplicity is the key to clarity.

● **Activity 5 Comparing styles** ●

Here are three extracts from the work of three different well-known authors. (You will find their names on page 000 but don't look to see who they are until you have completed the activity).

Read through the passages. Which do you find easiest to understand? Is the difference due to the *style* of writing or to the complexity of the ideas being discussed?

Extract 1

Private property is only the sensuous expression of the fact that man is both objective to himself and, even more, becomes a hostile and inhuman object to himself, that the expression of his life entails its externalization, its realization becomes the loss of its reality, an alien reality. Similarly the positive supersession of private property, that is, the sensuous appropriation by and for man of human essence and human life, of objective man and his works, should not be conceived of only as direct and exclusive enjoyment, as possession and having. Man appropriates his universal being in a universal manner, as a whole man. Each of his human relationships to the world—seeing, hearing, smell, tasting, feeling, thinking, contemplating, feeling, willing, acting, loving—in short all the organs of his individuality, just as the organs whose form is a directly communal one, are in their objective action, or their relation to the object, the appropriation of this object. The appropriation of human reality, their relationship to the object, is the confirmation of human reality. It is therefore as manifold as the determinations and activities of human nature. It is human effectiveness and suffering, for suffering, understood in the human sense, is an enjoyment of the self for man.

Extract 2

No society in which these liberties are not, on the whole, respected is free, whatever may be its form of government; and none is completely free in which they do not exist absolute and unqualified. The only freedom which deserves the name is that of pursuing our own good in our own way, so long as we do not attempt to deprive others of theirs, or impede their efforts to obtain it. Each is the proper guardian of his own health, whether bodily or mental and spiritual. Mankind are greater gainers by suffering each other to live as seems good to themselves than by compelling each to live as seems good to the rest.

Extract 3

The world has become the victim of dogmatic political creeds, of which, in our day, the most powerful are capitalism and communism. I do not believe that either, in a dogmatic and unmitigated form, offers a cure for preventible evils. Capitalism gives opportunity of initiative to a few; communism could (though it does not in fact) provide a servile kind of security for all. But if people can rid themselves of the influence of unduly simple theories and the strife that they engender, it will be possible, by a wise use of scientific technique, to provide both opportunity for all and security for all. Unfortunately our political theories are less intelligent than our science, and we have not yet learnt how to make use of our knowledge and our skill in the ways that will do most to make life happy and even glorious. It is not only the experience and the fear of war that oppresses mankind, though this is perhaps the greatest of all the evils of our time. We are oppressed also by the great impersonal forces that govern our daily life, making us still slaves of circumstance though no longer slaves in law. This need not be the case. It has come about through the worship of false gods. Energetic men have worshipped power rather than simple happiness and friendliness; men of less energy have acquiesced, or have been deceived by a wrong diagnosis of the sources of sorrow.

Now if you find the first passage difficult to understand you may be asking yourself, 'Is it me, or the author?' I would say that the trouble lies with the author, who makes himself difficult to understand in three ways.

First, he uses a lot of very long sentences – just look at the length of the first two. Second, he takes everyday words and gives them specialised meanings of his own. Only when you know what he means by, say, reality, can you understand his argument. And third, he gives no examples, preferring to write in a very abstract style.

The second piece is much easier to understand. Why? The ideas are comparable to the ideas in the first piece – both authors are discussing man's relationship to other men. Yet this author uses slightly shorter sentences and much simpler language. He uses everyday words to put over his ideas.

The third author is also very easy to understand. His sentences are simple and straightforward, his language clear and the whole passage flows from one sentence to the next. He knows how to use very short sentences – look at 'This need not be the case,' – as well as longer ones.

Now is it that the first author was very clever, the next clever and the last just ordinary? That I must leave you to judge for yourself, but if you now turn to page 87 you will find that all three authors are great men whose ideas and writings have influenced millions.

5.6 PARAGRAPHS

Each paragraph usually deals with one idea or statement. The logic of your outline is carried through by the logic of your paragraphs. If you are not certain which idea or statement one particular paragraph expounds, scrap that paragraph. For if you can't even understand the order of your argument, your readers don't stand a chance.

● **Activity 6 Paragraphing** ●

Here is a part of an article from the *Guardian* newspaper of 15 May 1980 printed not as it originally appeared but all as one paragraph. There were originally four paragraphs. Where did they start and stop?

Afghanistan called on Moscow and Washington yesterday to guarantee its relations with Iran and Pakistan and, for the first time, broached the possibility of a withdrawal of Soviet forces from its territory, the official Soviet news agency, Tass, reported. Tass quoted a Kabul government statement which said that the question of a Soviet withdrawal 'must be solved.' In Vienna, Chancellor Bruno Kreisky of Austria said that Britain's proposal for a solution to the Afghanistan crisis is a non-starter. In an interview yesterday he argued that it was unrealistic to consider that international guarantees for a neutral and non-aligned

Afghanistan, which form the basis of Lord Carrington's proposals, could persuade the Soviet Union to withdraw its troops. The Afghanistan statement opened by proposing separate talks with Iran and Pakistan, aimed at producing bilateral agreements to govern their relations.

There are actually three distinct ideas here:
(i) What Afghanistan said in a general sense.
(ii) Chancellor Bruno Kreisky's comments on the British proposal.
(iii) A more detailed treatment of the content of the Afghanistan statement.

You probably therefore guessed that one paragraph started with 'In Vienna' and one with 'The Afghanistan statement'. If you worked that out then you understand paragraphing very well. So where was the third break to make the fourth paragraph?

It came as 'Tass quoted', which illustrates something about the role of paragraphing in different contexts. In a newspaper you want (usually) punchy, racy, prose. You therefore use, amongst other techniques, more paragraphs than are strictly needed. The 'Tass quoted' sentence belongs in paragraph one. That is, it is part of the idea in paragraph one. But the author (or more likely the sub-editor) has chosen to split the paragraph in an unnecessary manner. I must emphasise that what the author has done is not wrong in any sense, merely unnecessary. In your own writing what you should aim to do is to identify the *essential* breaks for paragraphs and make these first. You may then choose to make more breaks depending on who you are writing for, your style, the length of your paragraphs, and so on.

5.7 DIAGRAMS AND ILLUSTRATIONS

Certain schools of thought have discouraged diagrams and illustrations in essays. There is no virtue in using or not using diagrams. Your simple rule is to use whichever approach best explains your ideas. If a diagram is needed, insert it. If it is not needed, leave it out. For example, you might need to use illustrations in some of the following circumstances.

Essay subject	*Illustrations/diagrams that might be needed*
Chemistry	Formulae
	Diagrams of models
	Charts, tables
	Pictures of apparatus

Geography	Maps, Charts, graphs
Social sciences	Tables, charts Graphs
History	Maps, charts Tables Graphs

● **Activity 7 Illustrating your subject** ●

What types of diagram or illustration have you used in the past when writing essays on your subject?

What types of diagram or illustration do you think are appropriate to essays in your subject?

5.8 REVIEWING THE ESSAY

Finally, go back over the essay draft. Look especially for unnecessary padding: for poor ordering of the material; for points missed or glossed over.

Essay-writing summary

Rather than summarise what I have said, I leave the task to eight Italian boys with little education but lots of sense:

> To start with, each of us keeps a notebook in his pocket. Every time an idea comes up, we make a note of it. Each idea on a separate sheet, on one side of the page.
>
> Then one day we gather together all the sheets of paper and spread them on a big table. We look through them, one by one, to get rid of duplications. Next, we make separate piles of the sheets that are related, and these will make up the chapters. Every chapter is subdivided into small piles, and they will become paragraphs.
>
> At this point we try to give a title to each paragraph. If we can't it means either that the paragraph has no content or that too many things are squeezed into it. Some paragraphs disappear. Some are broken up. While we name the paragraphs we discuss their logical order, until an outline is born. With the outline set, we reorganise all the piles to follow its pattern.
>
> We take the first pile, spread the sheets on the table, and we find the sequence for them. And so we begin to put down a first draft of the text. We duplicate that part so that we each can have a copy in front of

us. Then, scissors, paste and coloured pencils. We shuffle it all again. New sheets are added. We duplicate again.

A race begins now for all of us to find any word that can be crossed out, any excess adjectives, repetitions, lies, difficult words, over-long sentences, and any two concepts that are forced into one sentence.

We call in one outsider after another. We prefer it if they have not had too much schooling. We ask them to read aloud. And we watch to see if they have understood what we meant to say.

We accept their suggestions if they clarify the text. We reject any suggestions made in the name of caution.

Having done all this hard work and having followed these rules that anyone can use, we often come across an intellectual idiot who announces, 'This letter has a remarkably personal style.'

Why don't you admit that you don't know what the art of writing is? It is an art that is the very opposite of laziness.

(School of Barbiana, *Letter to a Teacher* (Penguin Books, 1970))

5.9 CHECKLIST

You should now find that you have:
   (a) Practised looking at essay titles in order to establish what is being asked for.
   (b) Practised writing essay outlines.
   (c) Reached your own conclusions on what makes a readable style of writing for an essay.
   (d) Practised paragraphing.
   (e) Considered the types of diagram or illustration that are relevant to essays in your subject.

CHAPTER 6

THINKING CLEARLY

6.1 WHY THINK CLEARLY?

A daft question? Perhaps it is for a student who has bothered to work through a course on study. But on the whole man prefers not to think clearly. The ability of governments to sustain futile wars such as World War I relies on the fact that subjects prefer slogans to ideas. It is easier to think all foreigners are dirty, ignorant or uncivilised than it is to learn foreign languages and study foreign cultures. It is easier to hold comforting beliefs with no rational basis whatsoever than it is to face the truth about man's humble position in the ecosystem. So on the whole we are not too keen on clear thought.

There are those, however, who hold the acquisition of knowledge to be good. Those who are prepared to think out their problems rather than accept clichéd arguments and hack solutions. For them the reward is great. Man's current mastery of the globe (albeit ill-used at times) has been achieved by thinkers. It is man's superbly developed capacity for thought that has enabled him to plan roads, transport, hospitals, schools, food and water supplies sufficient to cater for millions in days and years to come. These triumphs are not the product of random thought patterns. Only logical and appropriate thought patterns can achieve such successes.

There is, of course, no rational basis for preferring rational to irrational thought. Ultimately it is a matter of values and of choice. Equally so, we are surrounded by evidence of the utilitarian value of rational thought and usually this is sufficient justification.

If you want to think effectively and clearly, you may have to make great changes. True, you can think clearly in one small field and fail in others. All of us have these areas within which we cease to be rational. In studying logic and the rules of thought we are fighting a hard battle against irrational tendencies. If you should be tempted to give up, remember this. Truly logical thought, starting from true premises, must lead to a true

'Truly logical thought, starting from true-premises, must lead to a true conclusion'

conclusion. Irrational thought, whether or not it starts from true premises, can only reach the truth by accident. The moral is simply: If you want to understand and master the world, learn to think clearly and start now.

6.2 FOUNDATIONS OF CLEAR THOUGHT

Quite what goes on in our heads when we think, no one knows. Biologists, psychologists and philosophers ponder such fascinating questions as 'Is it possible for a man to think without language and without images?' I shan't attempt to compete with them. Instead, let's take a look at your tools of thought. Try this exercise:

Think about something for half a minute.

Now you've done your thinking, ask yourself in what form you thought. Did you use words? Did you use images? Did you use symbols? Did you 'hear' sounds? Undoubtedly you must have thought with the aid of words or symbols or images. So it follows that your capacity for thought is closely tied to your capacity to use words, symbols and images. I say 'closely tied' rather than 'completely tied' simply because there are areas of uncertainty about thought. You know how it is when you think of something but 'can't quite explain it'. The 'thought' seems to be there but in some form other than words or symbols.

So your capacity to think is closely related to your capacity to use the thought tools invented by man: words, symbols (mathematical, scientific, musical), images and so on. Don't, therefore, expect any golden rules of clear thought which anyone can use however deficient in other areas such as language.

(a) Concepts, categories and definitions

Man thinks in concepts. A concept is a classification which helps us to understand the world around us. The idea of 'table' is a concept. You haven't seen all the tables in the world but, because you have a concept of 'table' in your mind, you can recognise a new table as a table at a glance. Not all concepts are so straightforward. How about beauty or sin?

At this stage you should notice two important points. First, a man forms a concept to help him think quickly and clearly. He doesn't have to describe every table to himself; he just thinks 'table'. Second, we form concepts to communicate and the success of our communication depends on the closeness with which our concepts agree. Thus a Tory and a Socialist can probably discuss fairly well where to site a table in a room. They agree on the meanings of the words 'floor', 'table', 'left' and 'right'. But when they want to discuss 'ownership' they soon get into a quarrel. And more than half the trouble stems from their using the same words to mean different things.

In everyday speech we are quite careless about the words we use and the meanings we attach to them. But ill-defined words preclude clear thinking. For example, at the time of writing, the Government and several newspapers are obsessed with the notion that 'trade unions are holding the public to ransom with their large wage demands'. But is it as simple as that? Aren't trade unionists also members of the public? Now because the Government and newspapers start with a woolly assertion, they are in danger of reaching a woolly conclusion. Remember how I pointed out that reaching a correct conclusion from a false premise or by false logic is a matter of chance. Thus, to continue our example, the Government is more likely to reach a sensible conclusion if it starts with this question: 'Why is it that trade unionists make wage claims of such a size that they can only push up the prices of the items they buy as members of the public?'

In the formal learning situation we try to avoid these pitfalls by clearly stating our definitions at the outset. The debater who objects when his opponent 'defines his terms' objects because he fears the truth which so clearly follows clearly defined terms.

Thus you must expect many books which you study to start with definitions. Make sure that you understand precisely what the author means by the words he uses. Then you can understand his argument. Equally so, watch out for ill-defined words which may lead to unjustified arguments and conclusions.

● **Activity 1 What do words mean?** ●
Read the following advertisement carefully. How many words are inaccurately used in order to overstate the virtues of the car?

The SAAB 900 Turbo
The culmination of thirty years of SAAB experience in building quality motor cars has produced this miraculous marriage between almost irresistible performance and an interior which can only be described as wickedly self-indulgent and tempting.

However, if temptation of this sort seems somehow immoral, let us subdue any guilt feelings with a few well-chosen facts. For most of the time you are on the road, the modest and efficient 2-litre engine powers the car without assistance. The Turbo charger is used only when you need its breathtaking acceleration for fast, safe overtaking.

Thus, in today's energy-conscious world the SAAB 900 Turbo has achieved the perfect balance between ecology and safety.

Not wishing to make the Turbo sound too utilitarian, your first ride will confirm a standard of luxury which you can expect from one of the truly outstanding executive cars of the '80s.

Generous, elegant seating, abundant space, a silent environment and a unique SAAB ventilation system which passes all air through a special filter preventing even small particles, such as pollen and dust, from reaching the interior.

This attention to detail, of course, extends to all aspects of safety; impact resistant bumpers, steel safety cage, headlamp wash/wipers are safety aspects that SAAB have pioneered. But consider the extra benefits of SAAB's front wheel drive. Apart from providing better road holding and handling characteristics, it also means extra space for three rear-seat passengers without the bulky propeller shaft tunnel that still adorns some of our illustrious rivals.

If you have decided to indulge yourself with one of the world's prestige cars this year, visit a SAAB dealer and allow him to tempt you with a test drive.

(extract from SAAB advertisement in the *Observer*, 4 May 1980)

I would particularly pick out five phrases. You may well have others, but mine are:

(i) miraculous: the word means 'caused by a supernatural agency or power'. Is this true of this car?

(ii) energy-conscious world: the *world* cannot be conscious of anything. Only people can.

(iii) perfect balance: there is such a thing in some areas of life, but is a perfect balance between ecology and safety possible?

(iv) silent environment: I haven't been in the car, but I doubt that it is silent.

(v) impact resistant: a carefully meaningless phrase.

You may well have found this a bit difficult. The advertisement reads all right when taken at normal speed, which indicates how easily we accept words which are inappropriately used or are stretched beyond their meaning. To go beyond the superficial meaning, which is what we are doing when we 'study' something, requires slow and patient work. Unfortunately many people in the business of creating persuasive arguments –advertisers, politicians, pressure groups – are relying on the fact that we *won't* ask what their words mean. Thinking for yourself means that you do question other people's arguments. And often you will start with, 'Do you really mean . . . ?' or 'What exactly do you mean by . . .'.

(b) Evidence

'I read it in a book' is often consdered as sufficient evidence for the truth of a statement. In study we must apply more rigorous standards if we are to discern truth from falsehood. We must abandon common justifications and subject all knowledge to the strongest possible scrutiny. This means abandoning such phrases as 'It's common sense'. It was once common sense to burn 'witches' and to believe that priests were in personal touch with 'God' from whom they received instructions to massacre people in war and to imprison the genius Galileo. Today's 'common sense' stands a good chance of being tomorrow's discarded superstition.

The search for absolute knowledge, for incontrovertible evidence, is the realm of the philosophers. The search for more accurate knowledge is the realm of the intellectuals; it is the aim of study. What education should produce, writes Bertrand Russell, 'is a belief that knowledge is attainable in measure, though with difficulty; that much of what passes as knowledge at any given time is likely to be more or less mistaken, but that mistakes can be rectified with care and industry'.

It is this sceptical distrust of all evidence and knowledge which you must try and cultivate in your studies. Leonard Woolf held this view most strongly: 'I think it to be, not merely my right, but my duty to question the truth of everything and the authority of everyone, to hold nothing as sacred and to hold nothing in religious respect'.

The scepticism of Leonard Woolf and the tentative view of knowledge of Bertrand Russell are essential attitudes for those who wish to understand critically rather than by rote. These aims, however, are not achieved by instinct. We develop them by fighting against a human tendency to prejudice, to unjustified inference and to set thought patterns. Without these latter tendencies we could not live our daily lives. We must in our day-to-day routine make assumptions. You see a man in the uniform of the police force. Naturally you assume he is a policeman. You see a milk bottle filled with a white liquid and you naturally assume the contents to be milk. Now strictly speaking the man only has the appearance of being a policeman and the bottle only has the appearance of containing milk. There would be occasions when you would demand more evidence. For example, you might have heard that criminals in your district had taken to posing as policemen. In such circumustances you would demand more than superficial appearance before accepting a man as being a policeman.

Thus the evidence you demand depends on the possible consequences of a wrong identification or conclusion. Much experimental work in psychology has confirmed something which we all suspect: that people ignore evidence which is contrary to their own ideas. And the more strongly they hold their ideas the more selective they are in reading the evidence. There are many everyday examples of this. Take the driver who objects to safety-belts. He pounces on the odd case where a life is saved through not wearing safety-belts but ignores the thousands of contrary cases which justify the automatic wearing of safety-belts. Similarly, nationalistic attitudes are maintained by concentrating on the undesirable behaviours of some foreigners and **attributing this (a)** to their being foreign and (b) to everyone of the nationality.

In study it is essential to work at all the available evidence in an effort to weight it up and reach useful conclusions. Thus when presenting an argument, say in an essay, it is not sufficient to bring in evidence which supports your argument; you must also consider evidence which is contrary, or apparently contrary to your argument. Unless you can show why you reject opposing evidence, your own argument will be unconvincing and open to the charge of bias.

● **Activity 2 Evidence** ●

Here are two leading articles from national newspapers. One was published on 17 May 1980, the other on 19 May 1980. Both followed the announcement that inflation during the first year of the new Tory Government had been 22.8 per cent.

Read the articles carefully. To what extent does each article cite *evidence* to support its argument?

Article 1

Last week's inflation figures, though widely forecast, produced the predictable shock-horror reaction on the part of posh-paper pundits, dial-a-quote trade union bosses – and Denis Healey.

The Prime Minister should ignore ALL of them. Especially Mr. Healey, who when HE was fighting inflation, managed to get the pound down to its lowest-ever level!

TRUE, the Retail Price Index HAS doubled in a year.

TRUE, our cost of living is the highest in the Western world. And there can be little doubt that inflation will get worse before it starts to get better.

That is bad. Very bad.

But we all knew it was going to happen.

PROBLEM

And free collective bargaining has ensured that for most people pay HAS kept pace with prices during that time.

The Government never claimed it could get on top of the problem in its first year of office. Indeed, their Election Manifesto said so in the most specific terms.

And Chancellor Sir Geoffrey Howe deliberately engineered the long-promised major shift from direct to indirect taxation knowing that it would put up prices.

None of this is new.

Remedies

So why all the siren voices suggesting a change of course?

It is altogether too soon to panic.

It is altogether too soon to disinter tired old remedies like a sudden freeze, a 'siege' economy or a huge increase in Government spending.

They have failed before, and will fail again. And there are no NEW remedies.

This is surely a time for Maggie and her Ministers to stand firm. To accelerate and intensify their carrying-out of the policies on which they were elected.

For the Government is open to criticism not on the ground that its economic policies have been shown to be wrong - they haven't - but that Ministers often seem to lack CONVICTION and URGENCY in pursuing them.

In *The Sun*'s view, the only hope for Britain's long-term prosperity is to continue with the present medicine, which is only just beginning to take effect.

We have to take the full course of treatment if we are to be cured.

Rewards

SURE, bad times are still ahead.

SURE, there are more 'shocks' - both real and bogus - to come.

But the rewards will far out-weigh the hardship. *If we keep our nerve.*

(*Sun*, 19 May 1980)

Article 2

High inflation, harsh deflation

Inflation is at 22 per cent, while the growth of the money supply is well within the Government's target range. These two facts speak volumes about the Chancellor of the Exchequer's economic policy. The first lesson is that four years of money supply control has failed to curb inflation. The second lesson is that the Government's overenthusiasm for its money targets may make the slump worse than the more sophisticated monetarists reckon it should be.

Our inflation is now the highest of all the major industrialised countries. It has more than doubled since the Government took office, though, ironically, inflation is the one thing the Government claims it can cure. Ministers certainly had bad luck in their inheritance from the Labour administration, and in last year's sharp rise in oil and other commodity prices. But over half of the acceleration in price rises is probably due to the Government's own policy of increasing indirect taxes, charges for public services and rents.

The economic ministers, of course, believe that limits on the supply of money will eventually control inflation, and the Chancellor has succeeded this month in reducing the growth of the money supply (M3) to within his target range. According to monetarist theory, the Chancellor should now be able to cut interest rates. But both he and the Prime Minister have refused to do so because bank lending – part of the money supply – is too high. This is very odd. As our financial editor has cogently pointed out, either the Government's policy is designed to control the money supply or it is not. If it is not, the Chancellor should perhaps announce targets for what he is trying to control.

The level of bank lending is, however, indicative of the ferocious squeeze on British companies from wage pressures and stagnant demand. That squeeze will be worsened by another example of the Chancellor's imperfect application of monetarist theory. In recession, the Government's tax revenues fall and its spending (on unemployment pay) increases, which automatically stabilises the level of demand for goods and services. Mr. Terry Burns, the Chancellor's Chief Economic Adviser, and his former colleagues at the broadly monetarist London Business School, rightly argued that the Chancellor should therefore allow the public sector deficit to increase and that it could do so without impairing the money supply targets. The Chancellor, however, ignored their advice, and his policy had thus needlessly deepened the coming recession.

He justified this decision after the event by the need to reduce interest rates, despite the fact that businesses will be hit harder by falling demand than by high interest rates. But now, ironically, the Chancellor is refusing businesses even the fall in interest rates that he wanted. Industry is being clobbered both ways, with the danger that Sir Geoffrey, in excessively deflating the economy, may now undershoot his monetary targets.

Much of the attractiveness of monetarist theory lies in its (dubious) claim that it can reduce inflation with only temporary loss of output or jobs. The Chancellor's behaviour, however, suggests that he has little faith that control of the money supply can affect price rises without sharp rises in unemployment. That deflationary policy is costly and ineffective, since no one can predict how high unemployment has to be before employees are scared into accepting lower pay settlements. At this rate, the Chancellor's Welsh fundamentalism will be giving the monetarists a thoroughly bad name.

(*Guardian*, 17 May 1980)

Article 1 is very weak on evidence. Indeed the author appeals to his readers to *ignore* any evidence that there might be. He says, 'It is altogether too soon to panic', when he clearly means that whatever the facts are they are not to be considered as evidence that the Government's policy isn't working. So this article is a good example of a form of emotional appeal that does not rely on evidence. It wouldn't get you many marks in an exam.

Article 2 on the other hand works hard at the evidence. It restates the Government's monetarist policy and what that is meant to achieve, i.e. that *if* money supply could be controlled, then interest rates and inflation will fall. The article then goes on to show items of evidence which indicate that the Government has achieved its monetarist target but not the good things that were suggested to go with it. Finally this article looks at evidence for the other claim of the Government's policy: that monetarism controls inflation without damaging industry or jobs. The article shows that this also does not appear to be the case and expresses fears for the future. Contrast this with the last two sentences of Article 1 which in effect say 'Stop thinking, don't look, and it will all come right in the end.'

6.3 SOME COMMON FAULTS IN THINKING

(a) The causative fallacy

The mistake here is in assuming that because A and B occur together, A causes B (or vice versa). Soap powder produces bubbles in water and cleans clothes. Consequently many people believe that the bubbles clean the clothes. In fact the bubbles play no part in the process and are not necessary to a good soap powder.

Another example of the causative fallacy is to assume that because B follows A, A is the cause of B. When this happens we say that the argument assumes *post hoc ergo propter hoc* (Latin for 'after this, therefore on account of this').

Proof that A causes B is much harder to come by than merely finding A and B occurring together or one after the other.

76

(b) Selecting convenient examples

One naturally looks for evidence to support an argument. Without support-
ing examples your arguments would be pretty worthless. But equally, unless
you look for and consider contrary examples, your argument may well fail
to take account of all the available evidence.

(c) Tautology

A tautology is basically saying the same thing twice over whilst giving the
appearance of an argument. Quite often the two parts of a tautology are
widely separated and difficult to spot.

(d) Exceeding your evidence

It is very easy to produce wonderful theories based on slim evidence.
Evidence leads us to set up hypotheses which we then go on to test. The
testing stage may be lengthy and require the collection of additional
evidence but at the end we hope to uphold or refute our hypothesis.

There are many everyday examples of how easy it is to go beyond
one's evidence. Consider observers of UFOs (unidentified flying objects).
UFO spotters correctly assert that UFOs are a common occurrence. Some
UFO spotters stop there; a few exceed their evidence to go on to talk of
visitors from other planets and so on. Mere existence of UFOs (which no
one can deny) does not justify the statements attached to them.

(e) Appeal to authority

It is very easy to assert in an argument that X must be true because
Professor Y said it. Such appeal to authority is dangerous and unreliable.
Provided Professor Y was talking on his subject, there is a reasonable
chance of X being true, but Professor Y's statement alone is not sufficient
justification. Professor Y's arguments must be tested just as severely as
anyone else's.

● Activity 3 Faults in thinking ●

All of the following statements are invalid in some way. Which of
the above faults (a) to (e) does each illustrate?

(i) 'People who are clever get high marks in intelligence tests.'
(ii) 'You should take more exercise – doctors say so.'
(iii) 'It's no use taking exams. I know a bloke with 2 'A' levels and
he's still unemployed.'
(iv) 'All this permissiveness has ruined the country. We used to be
top of the world when we had national service.'
(v) 'Fred must have a lot of money. Just look at that big new car
he's driving.'

(i) This is tautology. Intelligence tests are constructed so that people who are generally regarded as clever get high marks. The statement is therefore stating the obvious.

(ii) This illustrates the use of 'appeal to authority'. No *evidence* of the value of exercise is given. We are expected to believe it is valuable because doctors say so.

(iii) Here the speaker is selecting convenient examples. If he wanted to look at the value of qualifications and their usefulness in getting a job, he would have to look at *all* people or at a *representative* sample of people.

(iv) This is the causative fallacy. Because one thing follows another or happens at the same time as another, that is no proof that they are in any way connected. In fact proving that one thing is the cause of another is remarkably difficult, but that is not the subject of this book.

(v) Here the speaker exceeds his evidence. The fact that Fred is driving a big car is not disputed. But what can we deduce from that fact? Almost nothing without the aid of other facts. That Fred drives the car doesn't tell us he owns it, paid for it or rents it. Perhaps he's borrowed it or even stolen it.

6.4 WAYS TO BETTER THINKING

'Thinking is relating. Relating is seeking, and with reasonable luck finding, relations between the things we think about' (C. A. Mace, *The Psychology of Study* (Penguin Books, 1968) p. 87).

You have already met many aids to better thinking in the earlier parts of this course so here I am just adding in a few extra points. The following points are general guidelines. To be really effective they must be backed up by my earlier advice, particularly that on understanding in Section 2.5.

• Activity 4 Review Chapter 2 •
Go back to Chapter 2 and quickly review the summary boxes on pages 14 and 18.

Now that you have reviewed Chapter 2, I will add a few more hints towards better thinking.

(a) *Understand all the evidence and theories*
You can't hope to think clearly on a problem unless you have first mastered other people's arguments on the same topic. So the first step is to understand the subject matter you are working on.

(b) *Look for statements without evidence*
Once you are on the way to developing your own argument or line of thought you must back up all your statements with adequate evidence. Check through your argument to ensure that all your statements are backed by evidence.

(c) *Consider alternative evidence*
Your evidence is bound to be selective, check that it is a fair selection. Do this by:
  (i) listing the evidence you are using to support your case;
  (ii) then list any evidence which appears to contradict and conflict with your evidence;
  (iii) Finally, decide whether your argument and evidence need altering when lists (i) and (ii) are compared.

(d) *Look at your examples*
Quite often in an argument we cite examples to support our case. Look at your examples. Are they typical? Can you think of contrary examples? Are your examples too extreme?

(e) *Take your argument to its extreme*
Have you considered the logical extension of your argument? Take it to its extremes. This may reveal flaws in your argument.

(f) *Avoid emotional words and phrases*
An argument should rely on the relationship which you are able to develop between established facts – you show how one piece of evidence supports another and so supports your theory. Using emotional words and phrases must be avoided since they colour the facts and evidence in your argument. In courts, for example, the man in the dock is called 'the accused' – a neutral term (and a fact). To call him 'blackguard' or 'that criminal' would be to use emotive words which are not borne out by the facts, at least until the court has pronounced judgement.

(g) *Consider your topic from all possible angles*
Quite often we consider a question from one point of view only. Residents in the line of a motorway are only likely to see it as something which destroys their house and garden. But for clear thinking, each question must be viewed from all possible angles so as to avoid the bias of viewing from one position.

> **Ways to better thinking sumary**
>
> 1. Understand all the evidence and theories.
> 2. Look for statements without evidence.
> 3. Consider alternative evidence.
> 4. Look at your examples – are they typical?
> 5. Take your argument to its extremes.
> 6. Avoid emotional words and phrases.
> 7. Consider your topic from all possible angles.

6.5 CHECKLIST

You should now find that you have:
   (a) Practised looking at how some arguments rely on distorting the meaning of words.
   (b) Practised looking at an argument to see how well it is supported by evidence.
   (c) Practised identifying five of the common faults in arguments.

CHAPTER 7

REVISION AND EXAMS

7.1 REVISION

(a) Basic principles

Many students regard revision as something they do in the last week or two before their exams. Revision of that kind is simply cramming and is not to be encouraged. It violates the principles of understanding which I dealt with in Chapter 2. Instead of this last-minute cramming, attempting to learn material which has never been properly understood, your revision should be a regular process throughout the course.

Your revision should be an important part of your study timetable. I have already mentioned the value of revising each lesson at the beginning of a new study session. Extending this idea you should plan regular revision sessions like this.

    (i) Start each study session with a review of the last session.
    (ii) End each week with a review of the week.
    (iii) End each month with a review of the month.
    (iv) End each term (or three months) with a review of the course.
    (v) End your year's course with a review of the course.

In this way, each topic comes up for review five times. This allows you to reinforce your ability to recall the material and to review the connections you have made between the material and other topics. Your successive revisions counteract the forgetting curve (Section 2.2) and produce the effect shown in Figure 7.1.

After the first session, the ability to recall the learnt material quickly fades. The revision after one day immediately brings the recall ability back to 100 per cent. Then, through the first week, recall ability declines again – but not as rapidly as on the first day. This slower decline is the

Fig 7.1 *effect of revision on memorising*

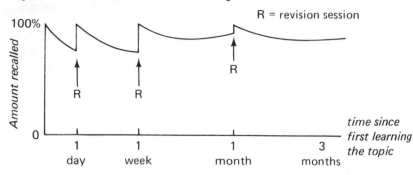

beneficial effect of the first revision session. So each revision session takes you back to 100 per cent recall and reduces the rate of loss of recall in the future.

(b) Characteristics of revision material

In ideal circumstances, the notes you made when you first studied a topic should be adequate for revision. That is, you shouldn't have to go back to your textbooks, lesson material and so on. In practice, your subsequent learning may lead you to wanting to alter your notes at one of your revision sessions. This can have beneficial side effects – for example, it can make the revision more interesting. But on the whole you should aim to make notes which will be suitable and sufficient for revision.

Having used your notes for your weekly, monthly and quarterly revision you may find them too full and lengthy for your final course revision. In that case your final revision can be partly based on making new, shortened notes. This has two benefits. First, the *act* of shortening the notes is an active form of learning. This not only promotes learning (see Sections 2.2, 2.5) but is also more interesting. Second, revision through shortening your notes provides you with a final condensed form of your material for further revision.

> ● Activity 1 Your revision notes ●
> Look at the notes you have used on a previous course.
>   Did you use the same notes from beginning to end?
>   If you have answered 'yes', did you find the notes ideal both for learning from and for revising from?
>   If you have answered 'no', how did your final notes differ from your initial notes?

(c) Methods of revising

With minor exceptions you should not be using revision sessions to learn new material or master new skills. Revision is simply going over material previously understood and memorised. If there are substantial parts of the course which you have not mastered you may well have to omit them altogether, rather than confuse your revision stage with new ideas and concepts. So try to keep your revision sessions as pure revision.

Although revising largely involves going over notes which you have previously prepared, it does not mean just passively reading through. Even at the revision stage you should be applying the ideas of Section 2.5 on learning so as to make your revision interesting and effective. For example:

Test yourself at regular intervals.

Try some problems which you haven't tackled before.

Write outlines for some possible essays.

Use active recall – reciting, reading or just verbal recall of your notes.

Talk about your subject with someone.

Check your understanding of your notes.

Ask yourself questions on your learning.

The main thing is to do something when you revise. This will help you to avoid the monotony of reading through your notes.

● **Activity 2 Making a revision plan** ●

Do part (i) of this activity if you are about to revise a course. Do part (ii) if you are not at the revision stage of any course.

(i) Make a revision plan for your course. This should include a rough schedule of what to do when. More important, it should include your list of ideas on *how* you are going to revise, the techniques and approaches you are going to use to make it interesting.

(ii) Look back at the revision methods that you have used in the past. Which were successful? Which unsuccessful and boring? What new techniques do you think you should use in the future?

Revision summary

1. Plan regular revision sessions in your timetable.
2. Revise from your notes. Improve them if necessary.
3. Avoid tackling new material in revision sessions.
4. Make your revision active – testing, writing, conversation, questioning.
5. Avoid passive reading of your notes.

7.2 PREPARING FOR EXAMS

At present many courses lead to exams so I can't avoid some notes on tackling them. I am not going to say a lot about this for one simple reason. By this stage of the course you should already know enough to take you through exams. That is, provided you successfully apply what you've already learnt to the whole of your exam course, the exam itself should prove no problem. But there are one or two additional points which you might overlook so I will deal with them here.

(a) Examining your exam

Long before you take your exam it is essential to know just what sort of exam it is. You will need to check on a number of points:

How many questions are there?

What type of questions? - essay questions, problems, factual listings, multiple choice, practical exams, oral exams.

How much choice will you have? This is very important if you can't finish the course before you start your revision. With sufficient choice you can safely omit one or two topics from your course.

> ● **Activity 3 What the instruction can tell you** ●
> What can you deduce from the following instructions which can appear on exam papers?
>
> (i) Answer only five questions.
> (ii) Answer in note form.
> (iii) Answer question 1 and three others.
> (iv) Answer all questions.
> (v) Tick the correct answer from the options given.
> (vi) Either . . . . or . . . .

You probably found those idiotically simple. So perhaps they are when you are not under the pressure of taking an exam. Yet thousands of people wrongly interpret such instructions each year and lose marks by doing so. So back to the questions. What can be learnt from them?

(i) Tells you that the marks are equally divided between all questions - if that were not so you couldn't be given a free choice of five questions. This instruction also tells you that to get full marks you must do five questions and that any answers after your first five are going to be ignored.

(ii) This tells you that there are no marks here for good English or well-phrased argument. It may also be telling you that there aren't many marks for this question and it is not meant to take up much of your time.

(iii) This tells you that you have to answer four questions to get full marks but that you have to answer question 1. It will be no use answering four questions if one of your four is not question 1. If you did that, only three of your answers could be marked.

(iv) This tells you that you *can't* assume that all questions carry equal marks so you have to do your best to cover all the questions. You have to try to avoid concentrating just on those you know best.

(v) This tells you that you only get a mark for a tick in the right place and that there are no marks for why you think that is the right answer. It is no use therefore putting notes at the side of your answer to explain it to the examiner. Those notes will be ignored but will have lost you time in the exam.

(vi) Full marks can be scored from either part. Since you may only answer one part you may not be marked on two. So if you answer both parts, only one part will be marked - usually the one that appears first on your answer paper.

(b) Practising for exams

However efficiently and effectively you have studied your course, exams will be different. The major difference is working to time. So practise at least two papers under strict exam conditions. (Most examining boards sell copies of old papers.) Allow yourself only the normal exam time and only those materials which you are allowed to take into the exam. This will also show you how much you can actually get done in the time and help you to plan your allocation of time within the exam itself. It will also reveal to you the extent to which you've mastered your course and it may show you that further revision and practice work is needed. For this reason make sure that your first practice exam is at least one month before the real exam.

● **Activity 4 Your past exams** ●

Have you ever done badly in a past examination?

If you have, to what extent was your exam preparation and technique to blame? Were any of these factors part of your difficulties?

(i) Too little revision.

(ii) Revising material that you hadn't previously mastered.

(iii) Not used to answering exam questions.

(iv) Ran out of time and so didn't cover the paper properly.

(v) Misread or misunderstood the instructions.

(c) The real examination

Preparing for this exam starts the day before. You must put ready everything you will need; pens, ball-point, drawing instruments, pencils, rubber, ruler, slide-rule, and whatever else you might need for your particular exam.

If the place of the examination is not familiar to you make sure you

'Allow yourself . . . only those materials which you are allowed to take into the exam'

know where it is and how to get there. Arriving late for an exam can ruin your chances of success.

Once the exam actually starts and you see the paper, pause. Too many candidates lose marks because they rush at the paper. First, read the instructions carefully, particularly with regard to how many questions you are expected to do. If you have a choice, look through the paper carefully. Put a light pencil line through those questions you can't possibly attempt. Put another mark (I always use a tick) at the side of those you can definitely do. Then answer the easiest (for you) questions first, leaving the doubtful ones to later.

Be careful not to over-answer. Each question should take no longer than the time allowed by the examiners but too often candidates take longer because they exceed the question. So, if a question is taking more than its fair share of time, reread the question – you may not be answering it.

Do remember that you can't get more than full marks on a question (and rarely as much as that). So a good pass requires answers to as many questions as the examiners tell you to answer. For example, suppose there are 100 marks, a pass mark of 50 and you have to do five questions. If you do three well (say 14 out of 20 for each) you get 42 marks – not enough to pass. But if you can get 4 out of 20 on each of two other questions you would pass. This illustrates an important point; if you haven't done your full quota of questions and are short of time, use that time to write short notes on the remainder of your quota. In this way you should be able to show the examiner more of your knowledge than by a more elaborate answer to one question.

Despite the best preparation, exams are a tense situation for anyone. In such situations it is all too easy to make silly slips. So do leave time to look over all your answers to pick out such mistakes. It's much better than belatedly remembering them when you've left the exam room.

7.3 CHECKLIST

You should now find that you have:
  (a) Made a revision plan for your course.
  (b) Reached a conclusion about the adequacy of your past methods of preparing revision notes.
  (c) Reached a conclusion about the adequacy of the strategy you use for taking exams.

ACTIVITIES KEY

Chapter 3, Activity 3

Time to read passage (minutes and seconds)	Reading speed (words per minute)
5 m.	148
4 m. 30 s.	164
4 m.	184
3 m. 45 s.	197
3 m. 30 s.	211
3 m. 15 s.	227
3 m.	246
2 m. 45 s.	268
2 m. 30 s.	296
2 m. 15 s.	328
2 m.	370
1 m. 45 s.	422

Answers to comprehension questions
1. (c)
2. (a)
3. (a)
4. (d)
5. (d)

Chapter 5, Activity 5

Extract 1: Karl Marx; David McLellan, *Karl Marx: Selected Writings* (Oxford University Press, 1977) p. 91.

Extract 2: John Stuart Mill, *On Liberty* (Watts & Co., 1929) p. 15.

Extract 3: Bertrand Russell, *Authority and the Individual* (Allen & Unwin; 1st ed. 1949; new paperback ed. 1977) p. 90.